THE IRISH BUCKET LIST

101 places to see in Ireland before you die

Stevie Haughey

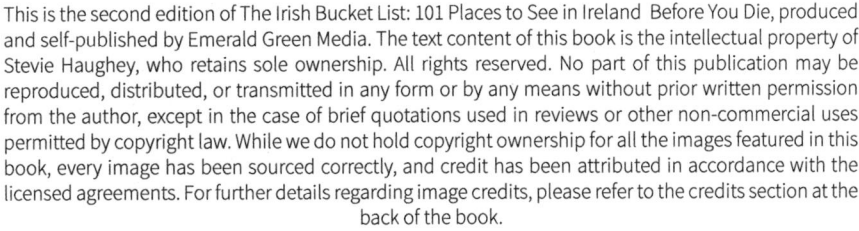

This is the second edition of The Irish Bucket List: 101 Places to See in Ireland Before You Die, produced and self-published by Emerald Green Media. The text content of this book is the intellectual property of Stevie Haughey, who retains sole ownership. All rights reserved. No part of this publication may be reproduced, distributed, or transmitted in any form or by any means without prior written permission from the author, except in the case of brief quotations used in reviews or other non-commercial uses permitted by copyright law. While we do not hold copyright ownership for all the images featured in this book, every image has been sourced correctly, and credit has been attributed in accordance with the licensed agreements. For further details regarding image credits, please refer to the credits section at the back of the book.

Front cover image: Dún Briste, Downpatrick Head by Mikołaj Pisula, licensed under CC BY-SA 4.0.

Copyright © 2025

MAP OF IRELAND

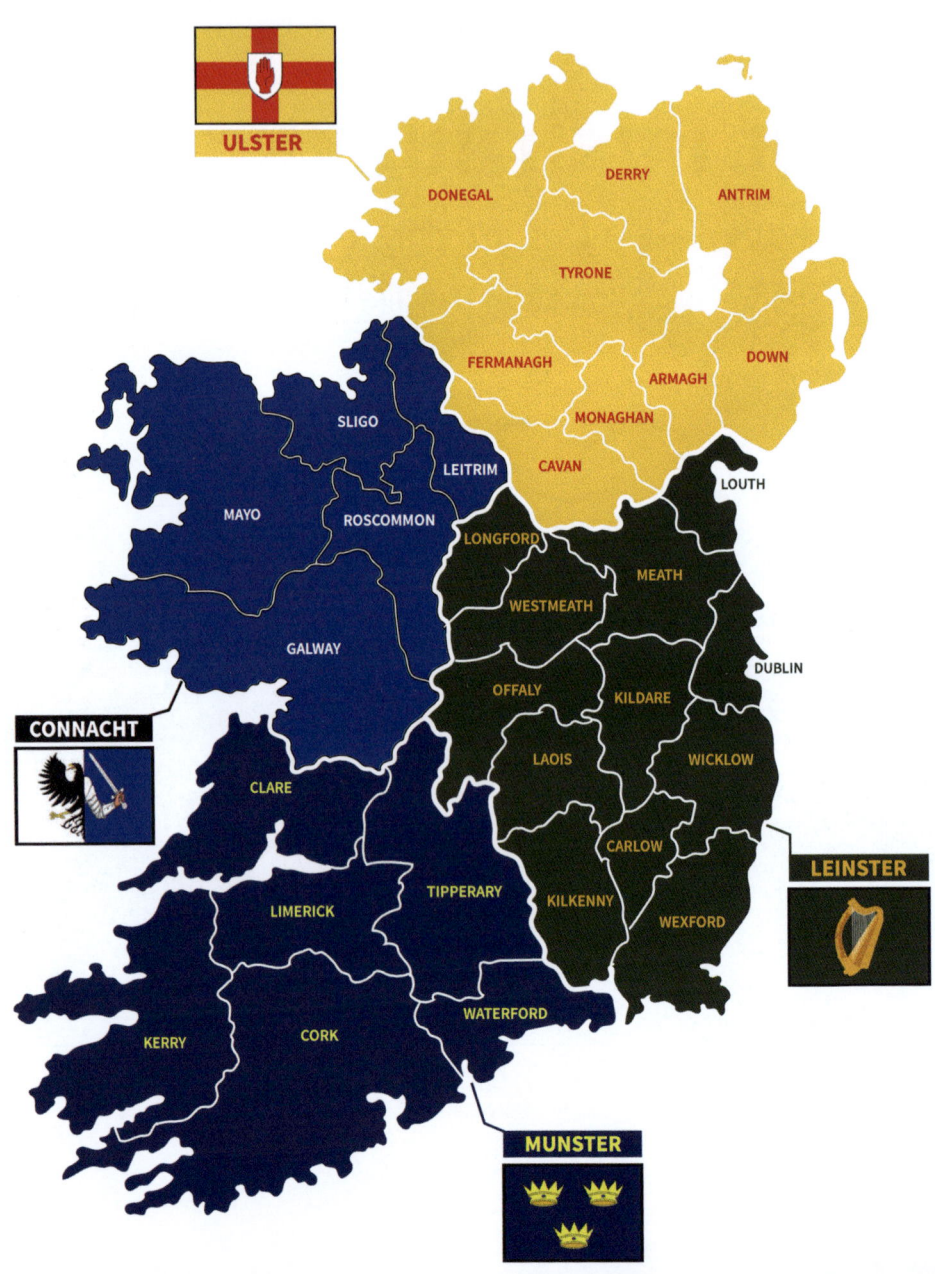

CONTENTS

INTRODUCTION	i - ii
ULSTER	1
Antrim	2 - 15
Armagh	16
Cavan	17
Derry	18 - 21
Donegal	22 - 28
Down	29 - 31
Fermanagh	32 - 33
Monaghan	34 - 35
Tyrone	36
MUNSTER	37
Clare	38 - 42
Cork	43 - 51
Kerry	52 - 57
Limerick	58
Tipperary	59
Waterford	60
LEINSTER	61
Carlow	62
Dublin	63 - 74
Kildare	75
Kilkenny	76
Laois	77
Longford	78
Louth	79 - 81
Meath	82 - 84
Offaly	85 - 86
Westmeath	87
Wicklow	88 - 90
Wexford	91
CONNACHT	92
Leitrim	93
Galway	94 - 96
Mayo	97 - 101
Roscommon	102
Sligo	103 - 105
IMAGE CREDITS	106

INTRODUCTION

When I left Ireland at the age of 19, I didn't think much about the land I was leaving behind. Like many young Irish people, I believed that opportunity lay elsewhere, and England seemed like the right choice for me. So, I headed across the water for university with the idea to eventually end up somewhere else in the world. However, the more time I spent away, the more I realised just how special home truly was.

While abroad, I noticed how fondly people spoke of Ireland and its people. Strangers would light up when they shared their experiences of visiting or talked about their Irish roots. It amazed me how many people from across the world seemed to know more about Irish landmarks and history than I did myself. Their enthusiasm made me feel proud – but also curious. I felt compelled to properly explore Ireland and understand it better for myself. The more I read and learned, the more places I wanted to visit.

It's true what they say: absence makes the heart grow fonder. Being away from Ireland made me fall in love with it all over again. I began to feel a sense of obligation. How could I call myself Irish and not have explored the incredible history, landscapes, and culture that shaped me?

When I returned home for summer break at 21, I decided to make a change. I had been writing down a list of the best places to visit in Ireland that I wanted to explore for myself. As I began my adventures, I was surprised to find that Ireland was even more beautiful than I had imagined. Each visit deepened my appreciation for my homeland. Whether it was the dramatic Cliffs of Moher, or the hidden gems tucked away in quiet counties, I ticked more and more places off the list. What started as a personal journey quickly became a passion project to rediscover Ireland and share its wonders with others.

I learned that some places were overrated while others were hidden treasures. Like any country, Ireland has its highs and lows. But overall, it is an incredible island with a rich history, vibrant culture, welcoming people, and breathtaking landscapes.

In 2014, that passion led me to create Ireland Before You Die, which started as a simple Facebook page showing places to visit in Ireland. The page was launched with no expectations and, to my surprise, it took off almost immediately. Within a week, thousands of people were engaging with posts about Ireland's beauty and offering travel inspiration.

Over a decade later, that humble page has grown into one of Ireland's most influential travel platforms. With over 700,000 followers and countless messages from people across the globe, it's clear that the magic of Ireland resonates worldwide.

After years of exploring Ireland, I published my first book, The Irish Bucket List, in 2017. It compiled some of the best places to visit and became a best-seller on Amazon. But as time went on, I realised it needed an update. New discoveries, hidden gems, and attractions were missing, while simultaneously, my experiences had grown. I knew I had to create a revised edition, one I could be genuinely proud of. And here it is.

I am privileged to have travelled to every county in Ireland, exploring its finest offerings and meeting incredible people along the way. This second edition is the culmination of everything I've seen, learned, and loved about Ireland, offering a fuller and more rounded view of its best bits. My hope is that this book will inspire you, whether you're planning a trip to the island – or simply dreaming of one.

This isn't just a list of places; it's a celebration of the experiences that make Ireland unique. From the rugged Atlantic coastline to the cobbled streets of historic towns, every location has earned its place. Some are iconic, others lesser known, but all are worth visiting.

I've included every county because there's beauty to be found no matter where you go. This is more than a guidebook, it's an invitation to explore, learn, and fall in love with Ireland as I have. Each entry provides just enough to spark your journey, leaving room for your own discoveries. For more details about any place, our website and other resources are there to help. This book is your starting point, your companion on a journey through the Emerald Isle.

Since launching Ireland Before You Die, I have fallen in love with the land all over again. I now live in Belfast and regularly travel around Ireland. I'm living the dream, exploring the land I love and managing a company that promotes it. I'm incredibly grateful to you for buying this book, and to everyone who has followed along and made my dream a reality.

Ireland has a way of leaving a mark on people. It's not just the stunning landscapes or the rich history. It's the warmth of the people, the stories in every corner, and the feeling that you're part of something timeless. My mission has always been to inspire others to experience that magic for themselves. This book is a continuation of that mission, and I'm incredibly proud to share it with you.

So, whether you're Irish-born, part of the Irish diaspora, or someone who has always been drawn to this island, this book is for you. Dive in. Let it guide you to places you've never been or remind you of places you've loved before. And above all, let it inspire you to explore Ireland, because these are the best places to see in **Ireland Before You Die**.

ULSTER

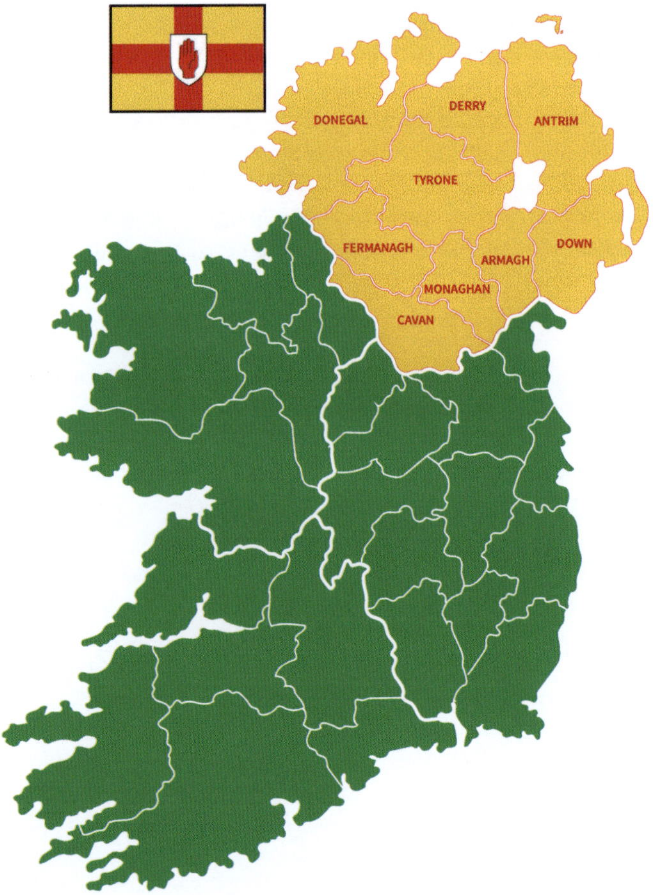

Carrick-A-Rede Rope Bridge

Cross Ireland's most iconic rope bridge, high above the Atlantic Ocean.

Beauty Score ★★★★★
Historical Score ★★☆☆☆
Cultural Score ★★★☆☆

OVERVIEW
Carrick-A-Rede Rope Bridge is one of Northern Ireland's top tourist attractions. The bridge is managed by the National Trust and spans 20 meters (66 feet). It is perched 30 meters (98 feet) above the sea below. The rope bridge is regularly checked and maintained to ensure safety, with a maximum of eight people allowed to cross at any one time. Visitors can enjoy a scenic coastal walk to the bridge, take in the spectacular views, and explore the area's rich history. The bridge connects the mainland to the small island of Carrickarade and provides an exhilarating experience.

TOP TRAVEL TIP
Wear sturdy shoes and hold on to your hat as you cross the bridge, as it can get windy!

WHY VISIT?
Walking across the Bridge offers a unique blend of adventure and stunning scenery, making it an unforgettable and very exciting experience for visitors of all ages.

FUN FACT!
Carrick-A-Rede Rope Bridge was originally built by the salmon fishermen over 350 years ago.

County Antrim

2

Causeway Coastal Route

Journey along Ireland's world-famous coastal route, a must-see for any traveller.

OVERVIEW
The Causeway Coastal Route is a bucket list-must for anyone visiting Northern Ireland. The route begins in Belfast and ends in Derry, passing through a series of stunning landscapes and iconic landmarks. Travellers can stop along the way and explore historical sites, enjoy delicious local cuisine, and experience the rich culture of Northern Ireland's coastal communities. Ideal for driving or cycling, with plenty of scenic viewpoints and hidden gems to discover, the Causeway Coast should not be missed!

BEST TIME TO VISIT
Late spring to early autumn (May to September) for ideal weather and extended daylight. Visit Monday to Thursday to avoid weekend traffic.

TOP FACT
The route includes the UNESCO World Heritage site, the Giant's Causeway, famous for its unique basalt columns.

TOP TRAVEL TIP
Take your time to explore the hidden coves, coastal trails, and local eateries along the route for a truly immersive experience.

Beauty Score ★★★★★
Historical Score ★★★★☆
Cultural Score ★★★★☆

WHY VISIT?
The Causeway Coastal Route offers an unforgettable road trip along Northern Ireland's breathtaking coastline. This 120-mile (193 km) stretch of road passes rugged cliffs, picturesque beaches, and quaint towns, providing plenty of opportunities for adventure and relaxation.

FUN FACT!
The Causeway Coastal Route is home to several filming locations from Game of Thrones. Some of the most famous include Ballintoy Harbour and Murlough Bay.

ACCOMODATION
Consider staying in coastal towns like Ballycastle, Portrush, or Cushendall for convenient access to the route's attractions.

County Antrim

Dunluce Castle

Explore the ruins of one of Ireland's most dramatic coastal castles.

FUN FACTS!
Dunluce Castle has been used as a filming location for several productions, including the TV series *Game of Thrones*.

The castle was abandoned in the late 17th century when it fell into disrepair as its owners relocated.

GETTING THERE
The castle is accessible by car, with ample parking available near the site. It is a short drive from Bushmills and the Giant's Causeway.

TOP TRAVEL TIP
Bring a camera and wear comfortable shoes to explore the castle's rugged terrain.

County Antrim

Beauty Score ★★★★★
Historical Score ★★★★★
Cultural Score ★★★★☆

OVERVIEW
Built in the 13th century, Dunluce Castle has a rich history filled with tales of battles, sieges, and shipwrecks. As the former seat of the MacDonnell clan, the castle played a significant role in Ireland's history. Today, visitors can explore the incredible ruins, including the remnants of the Great Hall, kitchens, and living quarters. While here, you can enjoy panoramic views of the North Atlantic while the visitor center offers detailed information about the castle's history and significance.

WHY VISIT?
One of Northern Ireland's most picturesque and iconic castles, Dunluce Castle offers a fascinating glimpse into the island's Medieval history. The castle's dramatic location on the edge of a basalt outcrop, surrounded by steep drops to the sea, offers breathtaking coastal scenery and a stunning backdrop for exploration and photography.

BEST TIME TO VISIT
Late spring to early autumn (May to September) for the best weather and longest daylight hours.

The Giant's Causeway

Walk on the world-famous hexagon basalt columns formed by ancient volcanic activity.

OVERVIEW
Set along the north coast of County Antrim, The Giant's Causeway is a must-visit for nature enthusiasts and geology buffs. Visitors can explore the dramatic landscape, walk along the winding coastal paths, and marvel at the natural beauty of this unique coastal location. For the ultimate experience, make sure you visit the state-of-the-art Visitor Centre, which provides tours and detailed information about the geological origins of the Causeway.

BEST TIME TO VISIT
Late spring to early autumn (May to September) for the best weather, clear views, and access to visitor facilities.

TOP FACT
The Giant's Causeway was decared a UNESCO World Heritage Site in 1986 due to its geological significance.

TOP TRAVEL TIP
Wear sturdy shoes for the walk and bring a rain jacket, as the weather can be unpredictable.

LOCAL LEGEND
The story goes that Finn McCool, the Irish giant, built the Causeway to cross the sea and battle the giant Benandonner, but fled back to Ireland when he saw how enormous his Scottish rival was.

Beauty Score	★★★★★
Historical Score	★★☆☆☆
Cultural Score	★★★★☆

County Antrim

WHY VISIT?
One of Northern Ireland's most iconic natural wonders, the Giant's Causeway is renowned for its extraordinary rock formations and stunning coastal views. A geological marvel resulting from an ancient volcanic eruption, this causeway consists of about 40,000 interlocking basalt columns, making it a truly unique attraction you don't want to miss.

GETTING THERE
The Causeway is accessible by car or public transport from nearby towns like Bushmills and Coleraine.

Glenoe Waterfall

Visit one of Ireland's most picturesque and secluded waterfalls.

OVERVIEW

Nestled in the small village of Glenoe, this enchanting waterfall is a hidden treasure in the countryside of County Antrim. Managed by the National Trust, the waterfall is surrounded by a well-maintained path and viewing platforms, so visitors can safely enjoy its majestic natural beauty. The area around the waterfall is rich in flora and fauna, providing a lovely setting for a leisurely stroll or a peaceful picnic.

WHY VISIT?

Glenoe Waterfall offers a hidden retreat into nature, perfect for a relaxing day trip from Belfast. This peaceful and charming spot is ideal for nature lovers, photographers, and those looking to escape the hustle and bustle of busy city life. Accessible for visitors of all ages and abilities, you can get to the waterfall via a very short scenic and serene walk.

FUN FACT!

Glenoe Waterfall has been a popular spot for local artists and photographers, capturing its timeless beauty through various art forms.

Beauty Score ★★★★★
Historical Score ★★★★★
Cultural Score ★★★★★

GETTING THERE

The waterfall is accessible by car from Belfast (40 minutes) and Larne (10 minutes). There's a small car park located near the entrance to the walking path that leads to the waterfall.

ACCOMMODATION TIPS

Stay in nearby Larne or Carrickfergus for easy access to Glenoe and other attractions along the Causeway Coastal Route.

County Antrim

Rathlin Island

The northernmost inhabited island of Ireland.

Beauty Score : ★★★★★
Historical Score : ★★★☆☆
Cultural Score : ★★★☆☆

County Antrim

OVERVIEW
A hidden gem off the northern coast of County Antrim, Rathlin Island is accessible only via a short ferry ride from Ballycastle. The island is famous for its wildlife and visitors can witness an array of puffins, plus other beautiful birds. You can explore the island's history at the Boathouse Visitor Centre, walk along its scenic nature trails, and enjoy authentic Irish hospitality in McCuaig's Bar.

BEST TIME TO VISIT
April to early August, coinciding with puffin nesting season near the RSPB Rathlin West Light Seabird Centre.

TOP FACT
Rathlin Island is the northernmost inhabited island of Ireland, offering a peaceful retreat with its rugged landscape and serene environment.

ACCOMODATION TIPS
Ensure you book accommodation before visiting, as it is a small island with limited options.

LOCAL LEGEND
Rathlin Island is steeped in history and legend, including stories of Viking raids and tales of Robert the Bruce, who is said to have taken refuge in a cave on the island.

WHY VISIT?
Rathlin Island offers a perfect weekend escape from city life, renowned for its large seabird colony, dramatic cliffs, and serene landscapes. Visitors can explore rugged coastlines, enjoy breathtaking views, and experience unique cultural heritage.

GETTING THERE
The island is accessible by ferry from Ballycastle.
It is recommended that you pre-book your tickets, especially during the summer.

FUN FACT!
Rathlin Island is home to Northern Ireland's largest seabird colony, making it a significant destination for birdwatchers.

The Dark Hedges

Lose yourself in the mystical atmosphere of Ireland's most famous tree tunnel.

WHY VISIT?
A captivating and unique road renowned for its mystical atmosphere and cinematic beauty, The Dark Hedges gained popularity after featuring as the Kingsroad in Game of Thrones. Visitors can stroll under the interlocking branches of ancient beech trees, enjoying a memorable experience that feels like something straight out of a fairytale.

FUN FACT!
The Dark Hedges served as the setting for the Kingsroad in *Game of Thrones*. You can spot the lane in Season 2, Episode 1.

County Antrim

Beauty Score ★★★★★
Historical Score ★★☆☆☆
Cultural Score ★★★★☆

OVERVIEW
The Dark Hedges is a striking avenue of beech trees that were planted on private land by the Stuart family in the 18th century. The trees were planted to create an impressive and grand approach to the family's mansion. It has become a must-visit landmark due to its beauty and feature in *Game of Thrones*. Located close to Ballymoney, visitors can enjoy a surreal walk in nature, where the trees' twisted branches form a natural tunnel, creating an atmospheric setting perfect for photography, leisurely walks, and immersing yourself in the area's rich history.

BEST TIME TO VISIT:
Spring and autumn when the light filters through the leaves, enhancing the magical ambience.

ACCOMMODATION TIPS:
Stay in nearby Ballymoney or the larger town of Ballycastle for a range of accommodation options.

TOP FACT
The beech trees were planted by the Stuart family in the 18th century to impress visitors as they approached their mansion, Gracehill House.

LOCAL LEGEND
Legend has it that the Grey Lady, a ghostly figure, haunts the avenue, disappearing as she passes the last beech tree.

The Old Bushmills Distillery

Visit Ireland's oldest licensed whiskey distillery, crafting whiskey since 1608.

WHY VISIT?
The Old Bushmills Distillery offers a fascinating journey through the history and craft of whiskey making. You can embark on a tour of the working distillery and learn about the intricate production process. While here, you can enjoy a premium tasting session of their renowned range of whiskies.

GETTING THERE
Accessible by car with ample parking available nearby. The distillery is also reachable via public transport from nearby towns.

FUN FACT!
The distillery produces around 4.5 million litres of whiskey annually, using water sourced from the nearby River Bush.

County Antrim

Beauty Score ★★☆☆☆
Historical Score ★★★★★
Cultural Score ★★★★☆

OVERVIEW
Nestled in the picturesque village of Bushmills, The Old Bushmills Distillery is the world's oldest licensed whiskey distillery, making it a historic landmark of Ireland's whiskey distilling tradition. It was established in 1608, and today, guests can enjoy informative guided tours that reveal the secrets behind the distillery's award-winning single malt and blended whiskies. The tour includes a visit to the mash house, still house, and warehouse, before concluding with a tasting session highlighting the unique flavours and heritage of the iconic Bushmills Whiskey.

BEST TIME TO VISIT
Year-round, but consider weekdays for a less crowded experience.

TOP FACT
The Old Bushmills Distillery produces around **4.5 million litres** of whiskey annually, using water sourced from the nearby River Bush.

ACCOMMODATION TIPS
Stay in Bushmills village or nearby areas like Portrush and Portballintrae for a range of lodging options.

LOCAL LEGEND
Legend has it that the distillery's founder, Sir Thomas Phillips, received a license to distill in 1608 from King James I himself, solidifying its prestigious history.

The Crosskeys Inn

Step into Ireland's oldest thatched pub, which is full of history and charm.

Beauty Score ★★★★☆
Historical Score ★★★★★
Cultural Score ★★★★★

OVERVIEW
Situated in the small village of Toome, The Crosskeys Inn is regarded as Ireland's oldest thatched pub. Established in 1654, stepping inside feels like travelling back in time. The pub still boasts many of its original features, including a traditional hearth and wooden beams. Renowned for its vibrant live music sessions, warm hospitality, and delicious local fare, this is the ultimate place to enjoy a quiet drink by the fire or tap your feet to traditional Irish tunes. An unmissable spot, The Crosskeys Inn offers a unique experience steeped in history and tradition.

BEST TIME TO VISIT
Evenings, especially on weekends, to enjoy live music and a lively atmosphere.

GETTING THERE
Easily accessible by car with free parking available. It is also reachable by bus from nearby towns, such as Ballymena and Magherafelt.

ACCOMMODATION TIPS
Stay in nearby towns like Ballymena or Antrim for a range of accommodation options.

WHY VISIT?
The Crosskeys Inn offers a unique glimpse into Ireland's rich cultural heritage. Known for its traditional thatched roof and cosy ambience, this historic pub provides the perfect setting for enjoying live traditional music, hearty meals, and a pint of Guinness. Boasting rustic charm and a welcoming atmosphere, it is a must-visit destination for anyone seeking an authentic Irish pub experience.

FUN FACT
The pub's thatched roof, a rarity in modern times, is meticulously maintained using traditional methods.

County Antrim

10

Carrickfergus Castle

Discover one of the best-preserved medieval castles in Ireland.

Beauty Score ★★★★☆
Historical Score ★★★★★
Cultural Score ★★★★☆

WHY VISIT?
Carrickfergus Castle is a stunning Norman castle set on the shores of Belfast Lough. Visitors can glimpse Northern Ireland's Medieval past by exploring the castle's interior, walking along its battlements, and taking in the spectacular views of Belfast Lough. Carrickfergus Castle also features plenty of informative displays and exhibitions and an impressive collection of 17th, 18th, and 19th-century cannons that bring its history to life.

GETTING THERE
Easily accessible by car or public transport from Belfast, just 11 miles (about 18km) away.

FUN FACT!
Carrickfergus Castle has featured as a filming location for several movies and TV shows, including the iconic HBO fantasy drama Game of Thrones.

County Antrim

OVERVIEW
Built in 1177 by John de Courcy, Carrickfergus Castle has played a key role in Ireland's history, enduring sieges and battles from the Middle Ages up until World War II. Set in the seaside town of Carrickfergus, history enthusiasts and families alike will delight in a visit to this impressive castle. Visitors can witness an impressive array of well-preserved structures, including the Great Hall, towers, and dungeons. The castle is also surrounded by a picturesque fishing harbour, making it an ideal spot for a stroll.

BEST TIME TO VISIT
Year-round, with summer months (June to August) offering the best weather for exploring the outdoor areas.

ACCOMMODATION TIPS
Stay in Carrickfergus town for easy access to the castle and other local attractions, with a variety of accommodation options available.

Black Taxi Tour

Experience a unique and personal tour of Belfast's historical and political landmarks.

Beauty Score ★☆☆☆☆
Historical Score ★★★★★
Cultural Score ★★★★★

OVERVIEW
The Black Taxi Tour is a unique way to discover the history of Belfast. Experienced and knowledgeable drivers will guide you through the city's most poignant and historical sites and offer insight into the city's turbulent past. The tours often cover key neighbourhoods such as the Falls Road, Shankill Road, and the Peace Walls, with stops at murals that depict the city's complex history. The drivers, often locals who have lived through The Troubles, provide a unique and personal perspective, making the tour as educational as it is engaging. This immersive experience is ideal for those looking to understand Belfast's political and social history.

BEST TIME TO VISIT
Any time of year, with morning or afternoon tours offering the best light for viewing murals.

GETTING THERE
Pick-up can be arranged from your accommodation or at a central meeting point in Belfast. Contact your tour provider for more details.

ACCOMMODATION TIPS
Stay in Belfast city centre for easy access to the starting points of the tours.

WHY VISIT?
The Black Taxi Tour offers an insightful and intimate exploration of Belfast's turbulent history. Focusing on its political murals, peace walls, and significant sites from The Troubles, you can take in this fascinating side of the city's history from the comfort of a classic Black Taxi. Led by knowledgeable local drivers, these tours provide personal stories and historical context that you won't get from a traditional guidebook.

FUN FACT!
Black taxis have served as an alternative to buses in Belfast, particularly during the Troubles when bus services were disrupted.

County Antrim

12

Crumlin Road Gaol

Explore the history and eerie atmosphere of Belfast's most famous Victorian prison.

OVERVIEW
Crumlin Road Gaol, also known as 'The Crum', is a 19th-century prison that operated from 1846 until 1996. Today, it is a popular tourist attraction where visitors can get a fascinating insight into Ireland's punitive history. During your visit, you can explore the execution chamber, the underground tunnel to the courthouse, and the prison cells. Guided tours provide in-depth stories about the lives of prisoners, the harsh conditions in which they were held, and significant historical events linked to the prison. Special events and paranormal tours held throughout the year add to the intrigue of this historic site.

TOP FACT
The prison is linked to the Crumlin Road Courthouse by an underground tunnel that allowed prisoners to be transported securely between the two buildings.

GETTING THERE
Easily accessible by public transport, with frequent bus routes from the city centre stopping nearby. Parking is also available on-site.

ACCOMMODATION TIPS
Stay in Belfast city centre for convenient access to Crumlin Road Gaol and other attractions.

Beauty Score ★★★☆☆
Historical Score ★★★★★
Cultural Score ★★★★☆

WHY VISIT?
Crumlin Road Gaol offers a fascinating and chilling insight into Northern Ireland's penal history. Visitors can take guided tours and learn all about the history of this Victorian-era prison, including notable inmates and infamous escapes. Wander around its halls and ominous walls to fully immerse yourself in what it would have been like to be a prisoner living inside.

FUN FACT!
During its 150 years of operation, Crumlin Road Gaol housed over 25,000 prisoners, including suffragettes and political prisoners during The Troubles.

County Antrim

Titanic Belfast

Discover the world's largest Titanic visitor experience.

OVERVIEW
Titanic Belfast is a world-renowned visitor experience located in the heart of Belfast's Titanic Quarter. First opened in 2012, it stands on the very site where the famous ship was designed, built, and launched. Every detail is thoroughly planned, including the building designed to resemble the ship's hulls. It contains nine interactive galleries that chronicle the ship's story, and visitors can explore the shipyard, walk through recreated rooms, and even experience a virtual ride through the construction of the Titanic. With its engaging exhibits and state-of-the-art displays, Titanic Belfast offers a profound insight into the history and legacy of the ill-fated ship.

Beauty Score ★★★★☆
Historical Score ★★★★★
Cultural Score ★★★★☆

TOP FACT
Titanic Belfast has welcomed over six million visitors from more than 145 countries since its opening.

WHY VISIT?
Titanic Belfast offers an immersive journey into the history of the Titanic, the iconic ocean liner which sailed from Belfast in April 1912. From its conception in Belfast to its tragic sinking during its maiden voyage, the incredible visitor experience offers a unique and fascinating insight into the story of this famous ship. With interactive exhibits, replica interiors, and extensive artefacts, you can embark on a captivating and educational experience suitable for visitors of all ages.

FUN FACT!
The height of Titanic Belfast's atrium is exactly the same as the real height of Titanic's hull.

GETTING THERE
Easily accessible by car and public transport. Titanic Belfast is also within walking distance from Belfast City Centre.

County Antrim

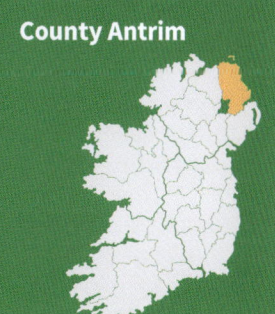

14

Galgorm

Experience one of Ireland's best luxury spa hotel, offering unparalleled relaxation.

WHY VISIT?
Galgorm offers a luxurious retreat with world-class spa facilities, beautiful gardens, and fine dining. It is ideal for those seeking relaxation, wellness treatments, and a touch of elegance, all set in a beautiful and historic setting.

FUN FACT!
Galgorm Castle, which dates back to the 17th century, is one of Northern Ireland's finest examples of the famous Jacobean architecture.

GETTING THERE
Easily accessible by car with ample parking available; also reachable by train and bus from Belfast to Ballymena.

TOP FACT
The Thermal Village at Galgorm Spa is the first of its kind in Ireland, offering a unique and extensive range of spa experiences.

Beauty Score ★★★★★
Historical Score ★★☆☆☆
Cultural Score ★★★☆☆

County Antrim

OVERVIEW
Galgorm is a popular luxury resort set in the picturesque countryside of County Antrim. The resort sits within 163 acres of parkland, which includes the historic Galgorm Castle and the award-winning Galgorm Spa and Golf Resort. The spa is famous for its Thermal Village, which offers outdoor hot tubs, saunas, and a range of therapeutic treatments. The resort also boasts several fine dining options, including gourmet restaurants and casual eateries that offer various culinary experiences. For golf enthusiasts, the Galgorm Castle Golf Club provides an 18-hole championship course with breathtaking views of the stunning surroundings. Whether you're looking to relax and rejuvenate or enjoy a round of golf, Galgorm delivers a perfect blend of luxury and leisure.

ACCOMODATION TIPS
Stay at the Galgorm Spa & Golf Resort itself for the full luxury experience, with a variety of room options from deluxe rooms to suites and private cottages.

Navan Fort

Explore the ancient seat of Ulster's kings and legends.

OVERVIEW
Located just outside Armagh city, Navan Fort is a ceremonial site that is believed to date back to 95 BC. Associated with the legendary warrior Cú Chulainn, it features prominently in Irish mythology. The site includes a large earthwork enclosure and a visitor centre to enjoy guided tours, interactive exhibits, and insights into the area's rich past. The peaceful rural setting provides an atmospheric experience.

BEST TIME TO VISIT
Spring to autumn (April to October) for the best weather and outdoor exploration.

TOP FACT
Navan Fort is the legendary home of the Red Branch Knights, the warriors of Ulster in Irish mythology.

TOP TRAVEL TIP
Visit the nearby Armagh Observatory and Planetarium for an added educational experience.

LOCAL LEGEND
Legends tell of the warrior Cú Chulainn defending the fort against invaders, adding a mythical dimension to the site's history.

Beauty Score ★★★★☆
Historical Score ★★★★★
Cultural Score ★★★★☆

County Armagh

WHY VISIT?
Navan Fort, or Emain Macha, is one of Ireland's most important archaeological sites. Steeped in myth and history, it has been the seat of many past Ulster kings. While here, explore the fort, learn about the Ulster Cycle's legends, and discover stories of ancient warriors, kings, and queens. The surrounding countryside offers breathtaking views, making it a fantastic spot for history enthusiasts and nature lovers.

GETTING THERE
A short drive from Armagh city via the A3 road.

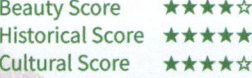

16

Dún na Rí Forest Park

Explore the enchanting woodlands and rich history of one of Ireland's most picturesque forest parks.

OVERVIEW
Nestled amidst a tranquil valley along the Cabra River, Dún na Rí Forest Park is a haven of natural beauty and historical intrigue. The park offers lush woodlands, diverse wildlife, and a network of walking trails that guide visitors through various historical and natural attractions. Highlights include the enchanting Fairy Glen, the romantic ruins of Fleming's Castle, and the scenic Martry's Lake. Whether you want to explore the great outdoors, discover local history, or simply relax in a beautiful setting, Dún na Rí Forest Park offers something for everyone.

BEST TIME TO VISIT
Spring to early autumn (March to October), when the flora is in full bloom and the weather is pleasant for outdoor activities.

GETTING THERE
Easily accessible by car, with ample parking available at the main entrance.

ACCOMMODATION TIPS
Consider staying in nearby Kingscourt, which offers a range of accommodation from cosy bed and breakfasts to luxurious hotels.

WHY VISIT?
Dún na Rí Forest Park offers visitors a chance to experience serene natural beauty, explore captivating woodland trails, and discover historical landmarks like Cromwell's Bridge and an ancient wishing well. It's perfect for nature lovers, history enthusiasts, and families looking for a scenic day out.

FUN FACT!
The park is said to be the inspiration for the setting of the famous Irish ballad 'The Valley of Slievenamon'.

Beauty Score ★★★★★
Historical Score ★☆☆☆☆
Cultural Score ★★★☆☆

County Cavan

Halloween in Derry

Experience one of the world's best Halloween celebrations with spectacular parades, fireworks, and vibrant festivities.

WHY VISIT?
The city of Derry is renowned as the host of one of the world's largest and most famous Halloween festivals. The city comes alive with spooktacular events, including haunted house tours, street parades, and live music, before finishing with a dazzling fireworks display over the River Foyle.

FUN FACT!
Derry's Halloween celebrations have been recognised by USA Today as the Best Halloween Destination in the World.

GETTING THERE
Accessible by car, bus, and train from Belfast and Dublin, with Derry's Eglinton Airport offering flights from various locations.

TOP FACT
The tradition of Halloween originated from the ancient Celtic festival of Samhain, and Derry embraces this heritage with its extensive celebrations.

County Derry

OVERVIEW
Halloween in Derry is a month-long celebration culminating in an epic Halloween night extravaganza. The city's medieval walls and historic buildings provide a perfect backdrop for the spooky festivities, and visitors can enjoy various activities, from ghost tours and storytelling sessions to costume parties and family-friendly events. The highlight is the Carnival Parade, featuring floats, performers, and incredible costumes, followed by the fireworks finale.

LOCAL LEGEND
Local folklore speaks of the ghost of the "Green Lady," who is said to roam the city's walls and historic buildings, especially during Halloween.

Beauty Score ★★★★☆
Historical Score ★★★★☆
Cultural Score ★★★★★

18

The City Walls

Walk along the best-preserved city walls in Ireland, offering a unique perspective on the city's rich history and stunning views.

Beauty Score ★★★★☆
Historical Score ★★★★★
Cultural Score ★★★★☆

WHY VISIT?
The City Walls of Derry are among the most complete and best-preserved city fortifications in Europe. Built between 1613 and 1619, they offer a fascinating journey through Derry's past, with panoramic views of the city and surrounding areas.

FUN FACT!
The walls have never been breached in battle, earning Derry the nickname "The Maiden City."

GETTING THERE
Accessible on foot from anywhere in the city centre, with several entry points along the walls.

ACCOMMODATION TIPS
Stay in the historic city center for convenient access to the walls and other attractions, with a range of hotels, guesthouses, and B&Bs available.

County Derry

OVERVIEW
Derry's City Walls stretch for approximately 1.5 kilometers (1 mile) and encircle the historic city centre. Visitors can walk the entire circumference of the walls, which are up to 8 meters (26 feet) high and 9 meters (30 feet) wide. Along the way, you'll find seven gates, 24 restored cannons, and several watchtowers and bastions. The walls provide insights into the city's tumultuous history, including the Siege of Derry in 1689, and offer picturesque views of the River Foyle, Bogside, and the cityscape.

LOCAL LEGEND
According to legend, the ghost of a young girl who died during the Siege of Derry still roams the walls, particularly around Butcher's Gate.

19

The Derry to Coleraine Train

WHY VISIT?
The Derry to Coleraine train journey is renowned for its breathtaking views of Northern Ireland's natural beauty, passing through picturesque coastal areas, lush green fields, and along the banks of the River Foyle. It's a relaxing and visually stunning way to travel between the two cities.

FUN FACT!
Michael Palin, the famous travel writer and television presenter, described the Derry to Coleraine route as "one of the most beautiful rail journeys in the world."

County Derry

Beauty Score ★★★★★
Historical Score ★★☆☆☆
Cultural Score ★★★☆☆

Enjoy one of the most scenic train journeys in Ireland, showcasing stunning coastal landscapes and rolling countryside.

OVERVIEW
The train route from Derry to Coleraine offers a spectacular 45-minute ride through some of Northern Ireland's most beautiful scenery. Starting from Derry's historic city, the train travels along the Foyle Estuary, offering stunning views of the river and surrounding countryside. It then skirts the scenic shores of Lough Foyle, passes through the atmospheric Downhill Tunnel, and provides glimpses of Mussenden Temple perched high above the cliffs. The journey is a perfect blend of history and natural beauty, ideal for both locals and tourists.

BEST TIME TO VISIT
Year-round, but late spring to early autumn (May to September) provides the best weather and visibility.

TOP FACT
The journey includes a passage through the Downhill Tunnel, which is 668 meters long and carved through a basalt cliff.

LOCAL LEGEND
Legend has it that the cliffs around Downhill were formed by a giant who hurled rocks into the sea during a fit of rage.

Mussenden Temple

Beauty Score ★★★★★
Historical Score ★★★★☆
Cultural Score ★★★★☆

WHY VISIT?
Mussenden Temple boasts breathtaking views over the Atlantic Ocean and Downhill Strand. It's an architectural gem set within the beautiful surroundings of the Downhill Demesne, making it a perfect spot for history enthusiasts, photographers, and nature lovers.

GETTING THERE
Accessible by car with parking available at the Downhill Demesne. The site is also reachable by train, exiting at Castlerock station, followed by a short walk.

FUN FACT!
Mussenden Temple is famously known for being perched precariously close to the edge of a cliff, a position that has continued to erode over the years due to the Atlantic Ocean.

County Derry

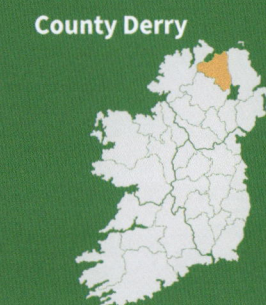

Admire the dramatic coastal views from one of Northern Ireland's most iconic and picturesque landmarks.

OVERVIEW
Mussenden Temple sits elegantly on a cliff edge overlooking the Atlantic Ocean. It is a small, circular building inspired by the Temple of Vesta in Rome. Built by Frederick Augustus Hervey, the 4th Earl of Bristol and Bishop of Derry, in 1785 as a summer library, the site is one of the most historical places in Northern Ireland. Part of Downhill Demesne, the temple's location provides panoramic views of the surrounding coastline, including Downhill Strand and Magilligan Point. Visitors can explore the temple, walk through the scenic grounds of the Downhill Demesne, and enjoy the tranquil atmosphere of this historic site. The site is managed by the National Trust and offers various walking trails and picnic areas.

Malin Head

Visit the northernmost point of mainland Ireland for dramatic coastal scenery.

County Donegal

OVERVIEW

Malin Head, situated on the Inishowen Peninsula, is the northernmost point of mainland Ireland. Famed for its stunning coastal landscapes and rich history, it offers breathtaking views of the Atlantic Ocean, the dramatic cliffs of northwest Ireland, and unique rock formations such as Hell's Hole and Banba's Crown. Malin Head has been a strategic point throughout history, from Napoleonic times until World War II. It is dotted with historical markers and relics that reveal the secrets of its history today. The area is also a haven for birdwatchers and wildlife enthusiasts, with frequent sightings of seabirds, dolphins, and even whales. Malin Head is a must-visit destination for those looking to experience Ireland's untamed beauty and historical depth.

Beauty Score ★★★★★
Historical Score ★★★★☆
Cultural Score ★★☆☆☆

WHY VISIT?

Malin Head is renowned for its rugged coastline, spectacular ocean views, and unique geological formations. It's a prime spot for wildlife watching, historical exploration, and experiencing the raw beauty of Ireland's picturesque Wild Atlantic Way.

FUN FACT

Malin Head was a filming location for Star Wars: The Last Jedi, adding a touch of cinematic fame to its natural allure.

GETTING THERE

Accessible by car with parking available. The site is also reachable by local bus services from nearby towns like Carndonagh.

Mount Errigal

Beauty Score ★★★★★
Historical Score ★★★☆☆
Cultural Score ★★★★☆

County Donegal

Climb the tallest peak in County Donegal for a rewarding hiking experience.

OVERVIEW
Mount Errigal, standing at 751 metres (2,464 feet), is the highest peak in the Derryveagh Mountains and the tallest mountain in County Donegal. Known for its distinctive quartzite peak that glows pink in the setting sun, Errigal offers hikers an unforgettable nature experience. Though steep and challenging, the climb is manageable for those with a moderate fitness level. From the summit, climbers are rewarded with spectacular panoramic views of the surrounding landscape, including the Poison Glen, Glenveagh National Park, and the Atlantic Ocean. Errigal is also part of the iconic Seven Sisters mountain range, making it a must-visit for those exploring Donegal's rugged beauty.

BEST TIME TO VISIT
Late Spring to early autumn (April to September) for the best weather and hiking conditions.

TOP TRAVEL TIP
Wear sturdy hiking boots and check the weather forecast before starting your climb, as conditions can change quickly on the mountain.

WHY VISIT?
Mount Errigal is renowned for its striking appearance and the breathtaking views from its summit. It is a popular destination for hikers and nature enthusiasts, offering a challenging yet rewarding climb.

GETTING THERE
Accessible by car with parking available at the base; located near the villages of Dunlewey and Gweedore.

FUN FACT!
Mount Errigal is known for its rapidly changing weather, which can add to both the challenge and the thrill of the climb.

TOP FACT
Errigal's quartzite peak often glows pink or golden during sunrise and sunset, creating a mesmerizing sight for photographers and nature lovers.

The Slieve League Cliffs

Experience some of Europe's highest and most dramatic sea cliffs.

OVERVIEW
The Slieve League Cliffs, located on the southwest coast of County Donegal, are one of Ireland's most spectacular natural attractions. Almost three times the height of the Cliffs of Moher, these towering cliffs are among the highest in Europe. Visitors can take in stunning views from the Bunglass viewing platform or hike along the cliff-top paths for a closer look at the dramatic landscape. The trail, known as One Man's Pass, offers a challenging yet rewarding hike with panoramic views of the Atlantic Ocean, Donegal Bay, and the distant mountains of Sligo. The cliffs are also rich in local history and folklore, adding to their allure.

BEST TIME TO VISIT
The Giant's Causeway was declared a UNESCO World Heritage Site in 1986 due to its geological significance.

GETTING THERE
Accessible by car with parking at the Bunglass viewing point; shuttle buses are also available from Teelin during peak seasons.

BEST TIME TO VISIT
Late Spring to early autumn (April to September) for the best weather and visibility.

Beauty Score   ★★★★★
Historical Score ★★☆☆☆
Cultural Score   ★★★☆☆

County Donegal

WHY VISIT?
The Slieve League Cliffs are among the tallest sea cliffs in Europe, rising nearly 2,000 ft (609.6 m) above the Atlantic Ocean. Visitors can enjoy awe-inspiring views, challenging hikes, and the sheer majesty of Ireland's rugged coastline.

FUN FACT!
On a clear day, you can see as far as the mountains of Sligo and Mayo from the top of the Slieve League Cliffs.

ACCOMODATION
Stay in nearby villages such as Carrick or Teelin, which offer cosy B&Bs, guesthouses, and local hospitality.

Ballymastocker Beach

One of Ireland's most beautiful beaches, famous for golden sands and stunning coastal views.

OVERVIEW
Ballymastocker Beach, also known as Portsalon Beach, is situated on the Fanad Peninsula in County Donegal. This expansive Blue Flag beach stretches for miles, offering soft golden sands and shallow waters that are perfect for swimming. The beach is framed by the dramatic backdrop of Knockalla Mountain, providing excellent opportunities for hiking and photography. The nearby village of Portsalon offers amenities such as a golf course, cafes, and boat rentals, making it the perfect location for a peaceful escape. Ballymastocker Beach is ideal for those seeking tranquillity and natural beauty away from the hustle and bustle of city life.

County Donegal

WHY VISIT?
Ballymastocker Beach, often hailed as one of the most beautiful beaches in the world, offers pristine sands, clear blue waters, and breathtaking views of the surrounding mountains and coastline. It's an ideal spot for relaxation, swimming, and scenic walks.

Beauty Score ★★★★★
Historical Score ★★☆☆☆
Cultural Score ★★★☆☆

FUN FACT!
Ballymastocker Beach was once voted the second most beautiful beach in the world by British newspaper, *The Observer*.

GETTING THERE
Easily accessible by car, with free parking behind the beach. The beach is also reachable by bus from Letterkenny.

TOP FACT
Taylor Swift visited this beach in 2021, sharing black-and-white photos of herself with the iconic footbridge in the background.

Glenveagh National Park

Beauty Score ★★★★★
Historical Score ★★★★☆
Cultural Score ★★★☆☆

WHY VISIT?

Glenveagh National Park offers visitors a chance to experience the rugged beauty of Donegal's wilderness. With its breathtaking mountains, pristine lakes, and ancient woodlands, there's plenty to see and discover. The park is home to the majestic 19th-century Glenveagh Castle and its beautiful gardens, and it provides ample opportunities for hiking, wildlife watching, and photography.

FUN FACT!

Glenveagh Castle was built by John George Adair, a controversial figure known for his harsh eviction of tenants during the 19th century.

TOP FACT

Glenveagh National Park is home to Ireland's largest herd of red deer and one of the last remaining breeding pairs of golden eagles in the country.

County Donegal

One of Ireland's largest national parks, renowned for stunning landscapes, historic castles, and rich wildlife.

OVERVIEW

Nestled in the heart of the Derryveagh Mountains, Glenveagh National Park spans over 16,000 hectares of stunning landscapes. The park features picturesque walking trails, scenic viewpoints, and the majestic Glenveagh Castle, which overlooks Lough Veagh. Visitors can explore the castle's beautifully furnished rooms and lush gardens or take a guided tour to learn about its fascinating history. The park is also a sanctuary for red deer and golden eagles, making it a paradise for nature lovers and wildlife enthusiasts. Whether you're hiking up Mount Errigal, strolling through the gardens, or simply enjoying the serene environment, Glenveagh National Park offers a memorable experience for all.

BEST TIME TO VISIT

Late Spring to early autumn (April to September) for the best weather and blooming gardens.

GETTING THERE

Accessible by car with parking available at the visitor centre and shuttle buses that run from the visitor centre to the castle. Public transport options include buses from Letterkenny.

LOCAL LEGEND

Local lore tells of the ghost of Cornelia Adair, the wife of John George Adair, who is said to wander the halls of Glenveagh Castle.

Tory Island

Discover the unique charm of Ireland's most remote inhabited island.

OVERVIEW
Located 14.5 km (9 miles) off the northwest coast of County Donegal, Tory Island is Ireland's most remote inhabited island. Known for its rugged beauty, the island is home to a small Gaelic-speaking community that maintains many traditional customs and practices. Visitors can explore ancient ruins, such as a 6th-century monastic site founded by St. Colmcille, the Round Tower, and Tau Cross. Tory Island is also renowned for its vibrant arts scene, which was spearheaded by the Tory Island School of Art. With its dramatic cliffs, crystal-clear waters, and abundant wildlife, visitors can experience a unique blend of natural and cultural attractions.

GETTING THERE
Accessible by ferry from Magheroarty or Bunbeg; the ferry service operates year-round but is weather-dependent.

BEST TIME TO VISIT
Late Spring to early autumn (April to September) for the best weather and accessibility.

LOCAL LEGEND
According to legend, the island was once inhabited by the Fomorians, a supernatural race defeated by the Tuatha Dé Danann in Irish mythology.

Beauty Score ★★★★★
Historical Score ★★★★☆
Cultural Score ★★★★★

County Donegal

WHY VISIT?
Tory Island offers visitors a rare glimpse into a unique island community off the coast of Ireland. With a rich cultural heritage, stunning landscapes, and significant historical sites, it's a haven for artists, birdwatchers, and anyone seeking a peaceful retreat.

FUN FACT!
Tory Island is ruled by a 'King' elected by islanders as part of an island tradition. This 'King' acts as representative, spokesperson, and cultural ambassador.

ACCOMODATION
Stay in one of the island's guesthouses or bed and breakfasts for an immersive experience in the local community.

Glenevin Waterfall

Witness the serene beauty of one of Donegal's most picturesque waterfalls.

OVERVIEW
The Glenevin Waterfall is located near the village of Clonmany on the Inishowen Peninsula. This beautiful 30 ft (9.1 m) waterfall is surrounded by lush greenery and can be reached via a well-maintained trail that follows the river's meandering course. The trail is suitable for all ages and offers several picnic spots, making it a perfect destination for a family outing. The waterfall is a serene sight, with its waters cascading into a plunge pool, creating a tranquil and picturesque setting. The surrounding glen is rich in flora and fauna, adding to the charm of this hidden gem.

BEST TIME TO VISIT
Late Spring to early autumn (April to September) for the best weather and to enjoy the lush surroundings.

GETTING THERE
Accessible by car with parking at the entrance; the waterfall is a short, easy walk from the car park.

TOP FACT
The pathway to the waterfall includes several charming footbridges and stepping stones that add to the picturesque journey.

LOCAL LEGEND
Local folklore suggests that the waters of Glenevin have healing properties, and many people visit to experience the refreshing mist of the falls.

WHY VISIT?
The Glenevin Waterfall is a stunning natural attraction that offers a peaceful retreat amidst the scenic landscapes of Donegal. Visitors can enjoy a relaxing walk through a picturesque glen leading to the waterfall, which cascades beautifully into a clear pool.

FUN FACT!
The Glenevin Waterfall was featured in the National Geographic Traveller's list of 'Must-See Waterfalls' in Ireland.

Beauty Score ★★★★★
Historical Score ★★☆☆☆
Cultural Score ★★☆☆☆

County Donegal

Mourne Mountains

Discover the majestic Mourne Mountains, a designated Area of Outstanding Natural Beauty.

OVERVIEW
The Mourne Mountains, located in County Down, Northern Ireland, is a rugged mountain range known for picturesque landscapes and rich biodiversity. The highest peak, Slieve Donard, rises to 850 metres (2,790 ft) above sea level and provides stunning views of the surrounding area, including the Irish Sea and even as far as Scotland on a clear day. The Mournes are crisscrossed with well-maintained trails, making them ideal for hikers of all levels. Highlights include the Mourne Wall, a 22-mile (35.4 km) dry-stone wall that traverses 15 summits, and the Silent Valley Reservoir, a tranquil spot for a leisurely stroll. The area is also famous for its diverse wildlife and rare plant species.

BEST TIME TO VISIT
Late Spring to early autumn (April to September) for the best weather and hiking conditions.

TOP FACT
The Mourne Wall, built between 1904 and 1922, spans 22 miles and was constructed to enclose the catchment area for the Silent Valley and Ben Crom Reservoirs.

Beauty Score   ★★★★★
Historical Score ★★☆☆☆
Cultural Score   ★★★☆☆

County Down

WHY VISIT?
The Mourne Mountains are renowned for their breathtaking natural beauty, offering a range of outdoor activities, including hiking, rock climbing, and cycling. The area is also steeped in myth and history, making it a perfect destination for adventure seekers and nature lovers.

FUN FACT!
The Mourne Mountains are said to have inspired C.S. Lewis's magical land of Narnia in his iconic fictional series, The Chronicles of Narnia.

ACCOMODATION
Easily accessible by car with multiple parking areas and trailheads; also reachable by bus from nearby towns like Newcastle and Newry.

Murlough Beach

Enjoy a pristine, sandy beach with stunning views of the Mourne Mountains and rich wildlife habitats.

OVERVIEW

Murlough Beach, located near the village of Dundrum in County Down is a long sandy beach backed by a large dune system. This beach is part of the Murlough National Nature Reserve, the oldest nature reserve in Ireland, established in 1967. The reserve boasts a variety of flora and fauna, including rare butterflies and birds, making it a haven for nature enthusiasts. Visitors can enjoy walking, birdwatching, and picnicking amidst the stunning backdrop of the Mourne Mountains. The well-maintained paths and boardwalks make exploring the dunes and the beach easy, providing a peaceful retreat for families and solo travellers.

County Down

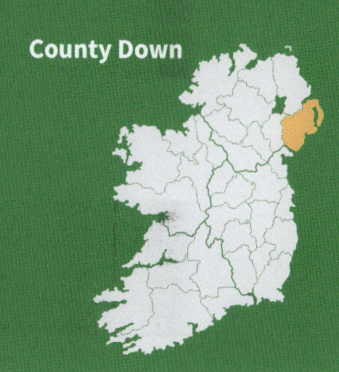

WHY VISIT?

Murlough Beach is a beautiful, unspoiled beach that offers a perfect blend of natural beauty, rich wildlife, and outdoor activities. It is part of the Murlough National Nature Reserve, renowned for its diverse ecosystems and scenic landscapes.

Beauty Score ★★★★★
Historical Score ★★★☆☆
Cultural Score ★★★☆☆

FUN FACT!

Murlough Beach and its dunes are home to over 620 plant species, making it one of Ireland's most botanically diverse areas.

GETTING THERE

Easily accessible by car with parking available at the Murlough National Nature Reserve; also reachable by local buses from nearby towns like Newcastle, Downpatrick, and Castlewellan.

TOP TRAVEL TIP

Bring binoculars for birdwatching and comfortable walking shoes to explore the dunes and the beach trails fully.

Mount Stewart

Discover one of Northern Ireland's most exquisite National Trust properties.

WHY VISIT?

Mount Stewart is home to beautifully landscaped gardens, a historic mansion filled with treasures, and several scenic walking trails. It's an ideal destination for garden enthusiasts, history buffs, and those looking to enjoy a peaceful retreat in a picturesque setting.

FUN FACT!

The gardens at Mount Stewart were nominated as a tentative UNESCO World Heritage Site in 1999 due to their exceptional horticultural importance.

GETTING THERE

Accessible by car with ample parking available; also reachable by public transport with buses running from Belfast to Newtownards and onwards to Mount Stewart.

County Down

Beauty Score   ★★★★★
Historical Score ★★★☆☆
Cultural Score   ★★★★☆

OVERVIEW

Mount Stewart is situated on the shores of Strangford Lough. A magnificent 19th-century mansion surrounded by world-famous gardens, the house is the former ancestral home of the Marquesses of Londonderry, a prominent Anglo-Irish family. The gardens are celebrated for their unique design and planting schemes, which feature various formal and informal garden areas, including the Italian Garden, the Shamrock Garden, and the Dodo Terrace. Inside the mansion, you can explore richly decorated rooms filled with family portraits, fine furniture, and historic artefacts. The estate also offers several walking trails providing stunning views of Strangford Lough and the surrounding countryside. Mount Stewart is a testament to the artistry of garden design and the rich history of the Stewart family.

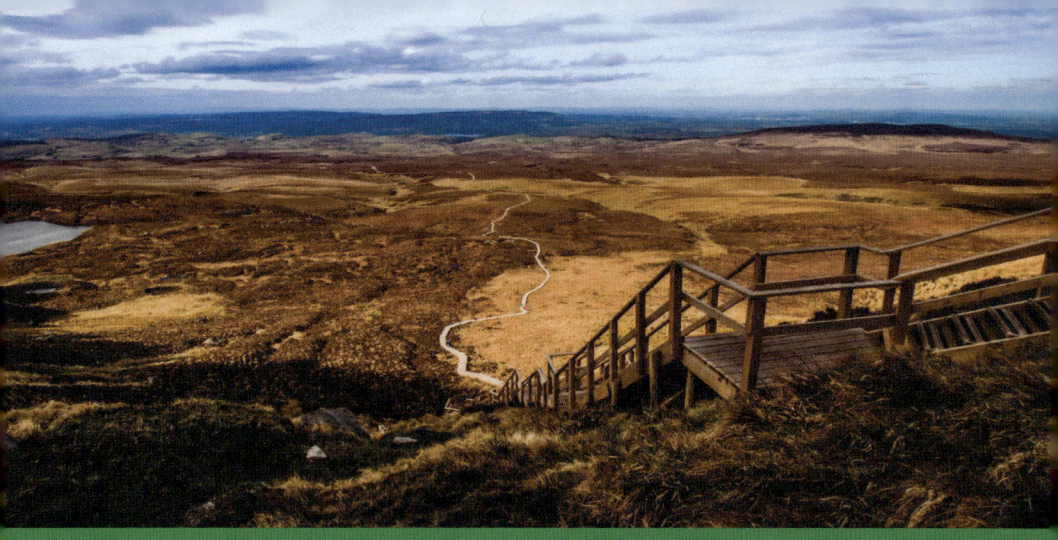

Cuilcagh Mountain Park

County Fermanagh

Hike the stunning 'Stairway to Heaven' and explore the unique landscapes of the Cuilcagh Mountain Park.

OVERVIEW
Cuilcagh Mountain Park, part of the Marble Arch Caves Global Geopark, is a haven for outdoor adventurers. The park's highlight is the Cuilcagh Legnabrocky Trail, commonly known as the 'Stairway to Heaven', a boardwalk that protects the blanket bog while providing a scenic route to the summit. The 7.4 km (4.6 miles) trail offers hikers spectacular views of the surrounding countryside and the chance to see rare flora and fauna. The park is also home to the Marble Arch Caves, one of Europe's finest show caves, which features stunning underground passages, rivers, and waterfalls.

Beauty Score ★★★★★
Historical Score ★☆☆☆☆
Cultural Score ★★★☆☆

WHY VISIT?
Cuilcagh Mountain Park is Ireland's only cross-border geopark, offering a breathtaking outdoor experience with its famous boardwalk trail, diverse wildlife, and dramatic landscapes. The area is known for its unique geology, ancient woodlands, and panoramic views, making it a must-visit for nature enthusiasts and hikers.

FUN FACT!
The Cuilcagh Legnabrocky Trail's boardwalk was constructed to prevent erosion of the delicate bogland, promoting sustainable tourism.

GETTING THERE
Accessible by car, with parking available at the start of the walk. Public transport is limited, but Enniskillen, 12 miles away, has good bus connections. From there, a taxi can take you to the trail.

Marble Arch Caves

Explore one of Europe's finest show caves with stunning underground rivers, waterfalls, and geological formations.

OVERVIEW

Located within the Marble Arch Caves Global Geopark, the Marble Arch Caves are an impressive natural attraction home to an extensive network of underground passages formed over millions of years. Guided tours take visitors through the caves, showcasing spectacular stalactites, stalagmites, and flowstones. The tour includes a short boat trip along an underground river, adding to the enchanting experience. The caves are part of a UNESCO Global Geopark, encompassing a diverse range of landscapes and natural habitats, making it a prime destination for geotourism and outdoor activities.

FUN FACT!

The Marble Arch Caves were formed around 340 million years ago during the Carboniferous period.

WHY VISIT?

The Marble Arch Caves offer a unique and fascinating underground adventure, where visitors can experience guided tours through magnificent caverns, winding passages, and tranquil pools. Along the way, you'll learn about this natural wonder's geological history and significance.

Beauty Score ★★★★★
Historical Score ★★★☆☆
Cultural Score ★★★☆☆

GETTING THERE

Accessible by car with parking available at the visitor centre; limited public transport options.

BEST TIME TO VISIT

Spring to early autumn when tours are most frequently available, and the weather is more predictable.

County Fermanagh

Castle Leslie

Experience the charm and luxury of one of Ireland's most enchanting castle estates.

OVERVIEW
Castle Leslie is located in the picturesque village of Glaslough and is one of the last great Irish castle estates still in the hands of its founding family. The estate spans over 1,000 acres of rolling Irish countryside with ancient woodlands and beautiful lakes. The castle offers a range of places to stay, including opulent castle rooms and charming village cottages. Guests can enjoy gourmet dining, relax in the Victorian Treatment Rooms, or participate in horse riding, fishing, and walking trails. The castle's rich history and family heritage add to its unique appeal.

WHY VISIT?
Castle Leslie offers a unique blend of historical elegance and modern luxury. Visitors can explore the beautifully restored castle, partake in various outdoor activities, or relax in the tranquil setting of the estate's extensive grounds. It's an ideal destination for those looking for a romantic getaway, a family holiday, or a luxurious retreat.

FUN FACT!
Castle Leslie was the venue for the marriage of Paul McCartney and Heather Mills in 2002.

GETTING THERE
Castle Leslie is best reached by car, with on-site parking available. Depending on your location, you may be able to take a bus to Glaslough or Monaghan Town, which is a 15-minute taxi ride away.

County Monaghan

Beauty Score ★★★★★
Historical Score ★★★★★
Cultural Score ★★★★☆

Rally School Ireland

Beauty Score ★★★★☆
Historical Score ★★☆☆☆
Cultural Score ★★★★☆

Experience high-speed master rally driving with expert instruction on world-class tracks.

County Monaghan

OVERVIEW
Located in the scenic countryside of Monaghan, Rally School Ireland provides a unique opportunity to learn and practice rally driving skills. The school offers courses and experiences suitable for all skill levels, from beginners to seasoned drivers. Participants can drive high-performance rally cars on specially designed tracks, learning techniques such as power slides, handbrake turns, and controlled skids. The school strictly emphasises safety while ensuring an exhilarating experience, making it ideal for individual bookings, corporate events, and group activities.

WHY VISIT?
Rally School Ireland offers an adrenaline-pumping adventure for motorsport enthusiasts and thrill-seekers alike. Visitors can enjoy hands-on driving experiences in rally cars, guided by professional instructors, making it an unforgettable day out.

FUN FACT!
Rally School Ireland has been in operation for over 25 years, making it one of the premier rally-driving schools in the country.

GETTING THERE
Accessible by car, with plenty of parking available on-site.

Ulster American Folk Park

Step back in time and discover stories of Irish emigration to America.

GETTING THERE
Easily accessible by car with ample parking available onsite. You can also reach via public transport with bus services from Omagh.

FUN FACT!
The park is home to the Mellon Homestead, the birthplace of Thomas Mellon, founder of the Mellon Bank in Pittsburgh, Pennsylvania.

TOP FACT
The park's Ship and Dockside Gallery features a full-scale replica of an emigrant sailing ship, providing a vivid depiction of the perilous Atlantic crossing.

Beauty Score ★★★★☆
Historical Score ★★★★★
Cultural Score ★★★★★

County Tyrone

OVERVIEW
The Ulster American Folk Park, located near Omagh, is an open-air museum that tells the story of Irish emigration to America. The park features over 30 exhibit buildings, including original and replica homes, schools, and businesses from both Ulster and America. Guests are guided through meticulously recreated streets and countryside, where they can interact with costumed interpreters and participate in traditional crafts and activities. The museum also hosts special events, such as the American Independence Day celebrations and the Bluegrass Music Festival.

WHY VISIT?
The Ulster American Folk Park offers a unique and engaging experience that showcases the journey of Irish emigrants from Ulster to America in the 18th and 19th centuries. Through an array of interactive and living history exhibits, guests can explore traditional thatched cottages, an emigrant ship, and American frontier settlements, all brought to life by costumed guides.

MUNSTER

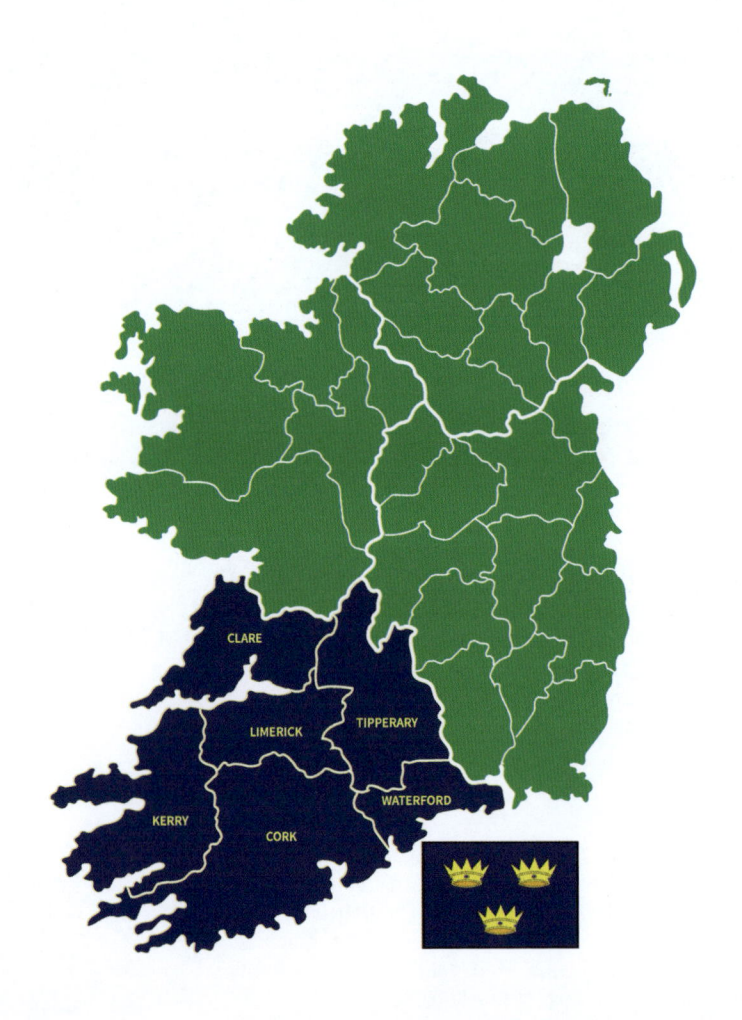

County Clare

Bunratty Castle & Folk Park

Step back in time to Medieval Ireland to explore a beautifully restored castle and traditional Irish village.

OVERVIEW

Bunratty Castle, a majestic 15th-century fortress, stands proudly in the heart of County Clare, offering a window into Ireland's Medieval past. Sitting adjacent to the castle, Bunratty Folk Park recreates an image of 19th-century rural Irish life, with thatched cottages, a schoolhouse, and a village street bustling with traditional old-school shops. The castle's grand halls, restored rooms, and beautiful tapestries transport visitors to another era, while the folk park's live demonstrations and interactive exhibits bring history to life. This family-friendly attraction is perfect for history buffs, cultural enthusiasts, and those seeking to experience Ireland's heritage.

WHY VISIT?

Bunratty Castle and Folk Park offers a unique blend of history and culture, allowing visitors to explore a 15th-century castle and a meticulously recreated 19th-century Irish village. An immersive experience that provides insight into Ireland's past, complete with costumed characters, traditional crafts, and vibrant gardens, Bunratty Castle and Folk Park is a fantastic day out for all ages.

FUN FACT!

The castle hosts medieval banquets with traditional music and entertainment, where guests can dine like lords and ladies of days gone by.

Beauty Score ★★★★★
Historical Score ★★★★★
Cultural Score ★★★★★

Cliffs of Moher

Beauty Score ★★★★★
Historical Score ★★★☆☆
Cultural Score ★★★★☆

County Clare

Witness one of Ireland's most iconic natural wonders and enjoy breathtaking coastal views.

OVERVIEW
Stretching for about 14 km (8.7 miles) along the wild Atlantic coast, the Cliffs of Moher offer the chance to experience some of the most spectacular scenery in Ireland. The cliffs also provide a vital habitat for various seabirds, including puffins and guillemots. While here, you can visit the award-winning Visitor Centre, which offers interactive exhibits, a virtual reality cliff face adventure, and a cafe with stunning coastal views. O'Brien's Tower, located at the cliff's highest point, offers an unparalleled vantage point. With paths and viewing platforms, the Cliffs of Moher provide an unforgettable experience for nature lovers, photographers, and tourists alike.

WHY VISIT?
The Cliffs of Moher are one of Ireland's most visited natural attractions, renowned for their dramatic cliffs that stand over 700 ft (213 m) above the Atlantic Ocean. Visitors can enjoy stunning panoramic views, abundant wildlife, and well-maintained walking trails stretching along Clare's west coast.

FUN FACT!
The Cliffs of Moher have been featured in numerous movies, including Harry Potter and the Half-Blood Prince and The Princess Bride.

GETTING THERE
The Cliffs are easily accessible by car, with ample paid parking at the Visitor Centre. You can also reach by bus from nearby towns and cities.

BEST TIME TO VISIT
Late Spring to early autumn (April to September) for the best weather and visibility.

Father Ted's House

Visit the iconic filming location from the beloved Irish sitcom Father Ted.

OVERVIEW
Glanquin House, located in the quaint village of Kilnaboy, County Clare, is the real-life residence used as the parochial house in the popular sitcom Father Ted. Nestled in the scenic landscape of the Burren, this house is a significant cultural landmark, and although it is a private residence, visitors can enjoy pre-arranged tours that provide insight into the filming of the series and the history of the house. During your visit, you can enjoy tea and scones while learning about the making of the show, making it a unique and memorable experience for fans.

WHY VISIT?
Father Ted's House, also known as Glanquin House, is a must-visit for fans of the hit Irish sitcom Father Ted. The house offers an opportunity to relive the most iconic scenes from the series while enjoying the picturesque surroundings of the Burren.

Beauty Score   ★★★★☆
Historical Score ★★★☆☆
Cultural Score   ★★★★★

County Clare

FUN FACT!
Despite being known as Father Ted's House, the show's interior scenes were actually filmed in a studio, and only the exterior shots were done at Glanquin House.

GETTING THERE:
Accessible by car, though you may need to park safely along the road. This is private property, and tours must be booked in advance. Entry without permission is prohibited.

The Burren

Discover one of Ireland's most unique and stunning karst landscapes, rich in history and biodiversity.

OVERVIEW

The Burren covers approximately 530 sq km (204.6 sq miles) in northwest County Clare. It is one of Ireland's most distinctive landscapes, characterised by its limestone rock formations and renowned for its unique flora, where Mediterranean, Arctic, and Alpine plants coexist. The Burren is also home to some fascinating historical sites, including the Poulnabrone Dolmen, an incredible portal tomb that dates back to the Neolithic period, as well as numerous ring forts and ancient churches. Visitors can explore the region via walking trails, guided tours, and visitor centres, offering insights into its geology, ecology, and cultural history.

WHY VISIT?

The Burren is a remarkably beautiful region known for its vast limestone pavements, rare flora, and ancient archaeological sites. It's a haven for hikers, nature enthusiasts, and history buffs alike, offering diverse experiences from botanical wonders to prehistoric monuments.

County Clare

GETTING THERE
Easily accessible by car, with multiple entry points and visitor centres; local bus tours are also available.

BEST TIME TO VISIT
Late Spring to early autumn (April to September) for the best weather and blooming wildflowers.

FUN FACT!
The name 'Burren' comes from the Irish word 'Boireann', meaning 'a rocky place', aptly describing its rugged terrain.

Beauty Score ★★★★★
Historical Score ★★★★★
Cultural Score ★★★★☆

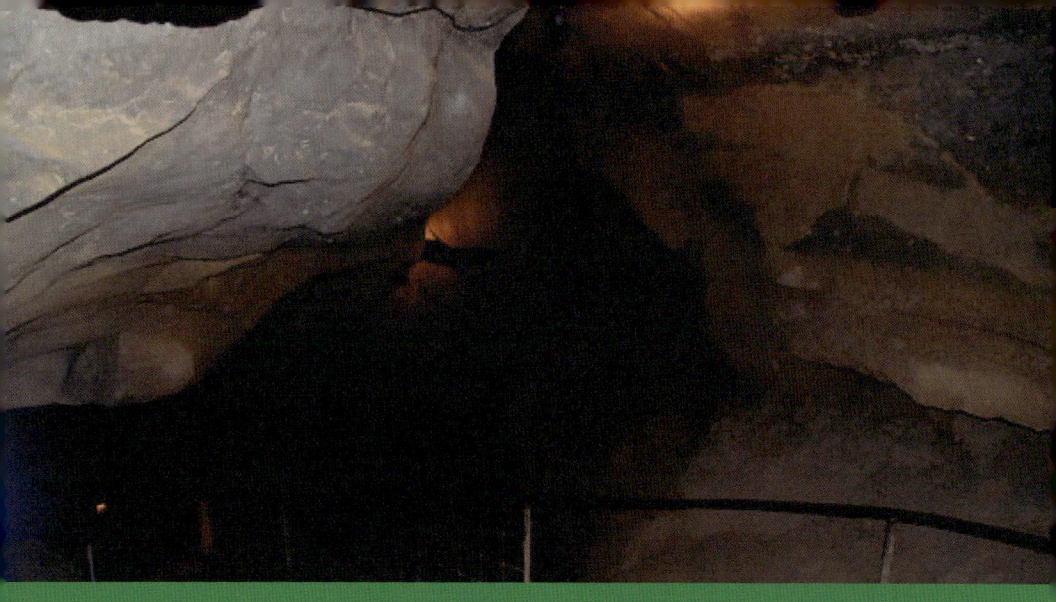

The Ailwee Caves

Explore one of Ireland's oldest and most fascinating cave systems.

County Clare

OVERVIEW

Discovered in the 1940s, the Ailwee Caves are part of the extensive limestone region of the Burren, one of Ireland's most compelling landscapes. Opened to the public in 1976, visitors today can take guided tours through the winding passages, marvel at the beautiful formations, and learn about the fascinating geological history of the area. The site also features a Birds of Prey Centre, a farm shop selling local produce, and a café that offers beautiful panoramic views of the Burren. The Ailwee Caves provide the perfect mix of adventure, education, and relaxation.

Beauty Score ★★★★☆
Historical Score ★★★★☆
Cultural Score ★★★☆☆

WHY VISIT?

The Ailwee Caves offer a unique underground adventure that is an exciting and educational experience suitable for all ages. Guided tours take you through stunning stalactites and stalagmites, an underground waterfall, and prehistoric bear remains.

FUN FACT!

The Ailwee Caves were formed by glacial meltwaters over a million years ago during the last Ice Age.

GETTING THERE

The caves are easily accessible by car, with parking available on-site. You can also visit as part of a local tour from Ballyvaughan.

Charles Fort

Beauty Score ★★★★☆
Historical Score ★★★★★
Cultural Score ★★★★☆

Explore one of Ireland's largest and best preserved star-shaped forts.

OVERVIEW

Charles Fort is located on the coast, close to the picturesque town of Kinsale. A prime example of a late 17th-century bastion fort, it was built between 1677 and 1682 to protect against naval invasions. It has played a prominent role in Irish history, including the Williamite War and the Irish Civil War. The fort's extensive grounds feature well-preserved ramparts, barracks, and defensive structures, offering a vivid picture of life in a historic military garrison. The fort also houses an informative visitors' centre with insightful exhibitions detailing its history. The stunning views of Kinsale Harbour and the surrounding countryside make it an excellent location for a scenic and educational outing.

WHY VISIT?

Offering a rich history and stunning harbour views, Charles Fort is a magnificent 17th-century star-shaped fort that provides visitors with a fascinating glimpse into Ireland's military history. You can also enjoy spectacular coastal views and explore the well-preserved architecture, making it a must-visit for history enthusiasts and photographers.

FUN FACT!

The unique star shape of Charles Fort was designed to resist cannon fire and provide a wide field of fire for defenders.

GETTING THERE

Accessible by car with parking available on-site. The Fort is also reachable by a scenic walk from Kinsale town centre.

BEST TIME TO VISIT

Spring to autumn (April to October) for the best weather and full access to the fort's outdoor areas.

County Cork

Dursey Island

Experience Ireland's only cable car ride to a remote and peaceful island.

OVERVIEW

Dursey Island is located at the southwestern tip of the Beara Peninsula. It is a hidden gem with rugged beauty and a serene atmosphere. Home to only a few residents with no shops, pubs, or restaurants, Dursey Island offers a peaceful retreat for nature lovers and hikers. Notable sights on the island include the signal tower and the ruins of Ballynacallagh Church. You will also have the chance to spot whales and dolphins swimming off the coast.

WHY VISIT?

Dursey Island offers a unique and tranquil escape with stunning coastal views, abundant wildlife, and a sense of isolation from the hustle and bustle of modern life. The island is accessible via Ireland's only cable car, adding a unique element of adventure to your visit.

FUN FACT
Dursey Island is connected to the mainland by Ireland's only cable car, which can carry six people and operates year-round, weather permitting.

GETTING THERE
Accessible by cable car from the mainland at Ballaghboy, near Castletownbere.

BEST TIME TO VISIT
Late Spring to early autumn (May to September) for mild weather and longer daylight hours.

Beauty Score ★★★★☆
Historical Score ★★★☆☆
Cultural Score ★★☆☆☆

County Cork

Spike Island

Explore the rich history of Ireland's Alcatraz, from its monastic origins to its time as a fortress and prison.

County Cork

Beauty Score ★★★★☆
Historical Score ★★★★★
Cultural Score ★★★☆☆

FUN FACT!
Spike Island was once the largest prison in the world, holding over 2,300 prisoners during its peak in the 1850s.

GETTING THERE
Accessible by ferry from Kennedy Pier in Cobh.

BEST TIME TO VISIT
Late Spring to early autumn (May to September) for mild weather and longer daylight hours.

OVERVIEW
Located in Cork Harbour, Spike Island is accessible via a short ferry ride from Cobh. The island's history spans over 1,300 years, having played significant roles in Ireland's religious, military, and penal histories. Visitors can tour the fortifications, explore the prison cells, and learn about the island's intriguing past through interactive displays and exhibits. Nature lovers can soak up scenic views of the harbour and surrounding areas.

WHY VISIT?
Spike Island offers a unique blend of history, nature, and adventure. The island has served as a monastery, a fortress, and one of the largest prisons in the world. Today, it is a fascinating tourist attraction with insightful guided tours, historical exhibitions, and beautiful walking trails.

The Blarney Stone

Kiss the legendary Blarney Stone and receive the gift of the gab!

OVERVIEW
Located within the enchanting Blarney Castle, the Blarney Stone sits high among the battlements. Visitors must lean backwards over a parapet to kiss the stone to gain the gift of the gab and honour a tradition that dates back centuries. Besides the famous stone, Blarney Castle offers beautiful gardens, intriguing rock formations, and scenic walks. The nearby village of Blarney is charming and offers additional attractions like the Blarney Woollen Mills.

WHY VISIT?
The Blarney Stone is one of Ireland's most famous attractions, drawing visitors from all over the world. Set within the historic and picturesque Blarney Castle, a visit to the Blarney Stone is as fascinating as it is unique.

FUN FACT!
Winston Churchill is among the many famous personalities who have kissed the Blarney Stone.

LOCAL LEGEND
According to local legend, kissing the Blarney Stone gives you the gift of the gab – the ability to talk with charm and confidence!

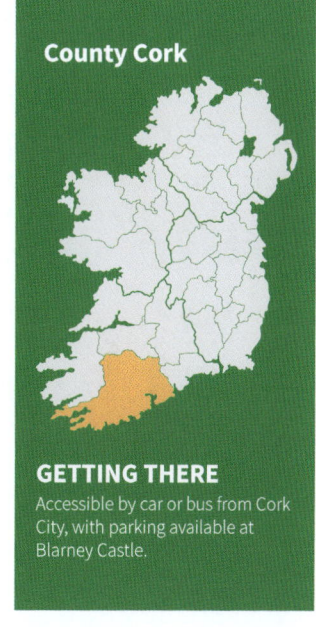

Beauty Score ★★★★☆
Historical Score ★★★★☆
Cultural Score ★★★★★

County Cork

GETTING THERE
Accessible by car or bus from Cork City, with parking available at Blarney Castle.

Cape Clear Island

Experience the culture, wildlife, and stunning scenery of Ireland's southernmost inhabited island.

OVERVIEW
Cape Clear Island, located 13 km (8 miles) off the coast of County Cork, is the southernmost inhabited part of Ireland. Renowned for its rugged landscapes, tranquil atmosphere, and rich biodiversity, the island is a peaceful haven for nature enthusiasts and cultural explorers. Visitors can explore scenic walking trails and historical sites such as the 5,000-year-old Dún an Óir fort. You can also find out all you need to know about the island at the Cape Clear Heritage Centre or visit its famous bird observatory, which attracts birdwatchers from all over the world. With a friendly local community and traditional Irish music sessions, Cape Clear Island offers an enriching and authentically Irish experience.

WHY VISIT?
Cape Clear Island offers a unique blend of natural beauty, vibrant Irish culture, and diverse wildlife. It is an ideal destination for birdwatching, hiking, and immersing oneself in traditional Irish life.

FUN FACT!
Cape Clear Island hosts an annual Storytelling Festival that celebrates Ireland's rich oral tradition and welcomes storytellers from around the world.

County Cork

Beauty Score ★★★★★
Historical Score ★★★★☆
Cultural Score ★★★☆☆

GETTING THERE
Accessible by ferry from Baltimore or Schull, County Cork.

Gougane Barra

Visit the picturesque birthplace of Saint Finbarr, the patron saint of Cork.

OVERVIEW
Nestled in a remote valley in the Shehy Mountains, Gougane Barra is an enchanting destination in County Cork. Famous as the home of St. Finbarr's Oratory, a small chapel situated on an island in the middle of a lake, surrounded by lush woodlands and rolling hills. Gougane Barra Forest Park offers numerous trails for hiking and biking, with breathtaking views and abundant wildlife to enjoy, making it perfect for those seeking solitude, natural beauty, and a touch of spiritual heritage.

WHY VISIT?
Gougane Barra is a beautiful and serene spot known for its stunning natural scenery, historical significance, and the idyllic St. Finbarr's Oratory, which sits alone on an island. The area offers a peaceful retreat into nature with its pristine lake, dense forest park, and ample opportunities for hiking and reflection.

TOP FACT
St. Finbarr founded a monastery at Gougane Barra in the 6th century, and the site has remained a place of pilgrimage ever since.

LOCAL LEGEND
According to legend, St. Finbarr built his monastery on the island in the lake at Gougane Barra, and it became an important religious centre in the early Christian period.

FUN FACT!
Gougane Barra is considered the source of the River Lee, which flows through Cork City.

GETTING THERE
Gougane Barra is accessible by car from Ballingeary or Macroom. Parking is available near the entrance to the forest park.

BEST TIME TO VISIT
Late Spring to early autumn (May to September) to enjoy mild weather and blooming flora.

Beauty Score ★★★★★
Historical Score ★★★★☆
Cultural Score ★★★☆☆

County Cork

Brow Head

Ireland's southernmost point offers breathtaking ocean views and historical insights.

WHY VISIT?
Brow Head is known for its stunning coastal scenery, rich maritime history, and remnants of historic signal towers. It offers a tranquil escape for hikers, history enthusiasts, and nature lovers alike.

GETTING THERE
Accessible by car with parking available in nearby Crookhaven; also reachable via local hiking trails.

FUN FACT!
Brow Head acted as a filming location for the 2017 movie Star Wars: The Last Jedi, adding a touch of cinematic fame to its historical significance.

TOP FACT
The signal tower at Brow Head was part of a series of towers built along the Irish coast during the Napoleonic Wars to warn of potential French invasions.

County Cork

OVERVIEW
The southernmost point of mainland Ireland, Brow Head, is located near the charming village of Crookhaven in County Cork. The headland is famed for its dramatic cliffs and panoramic views of the Atlantic Ocean. Visitors can explore the remains of an old signal tower, used during the Napoleonic Wars and later functioning as a Marconi wireless station. The rugged beauty and historical intrigue of this area make it a must-visit for those exploring Ireland's Wild Atlantic Way. The area also proves popular for its walking trails, which offer spectacular views and a chance to experience the raw, natural beauty of Ireland's coastline.

BEST TIME TO VISIT
Late Spring to early autumn (April to September) for the best weather and visibility.

Beauty Score ★★★★★
Historical Score ★★★★☆
Cultural Score ★★★☆☆

49

Cobh

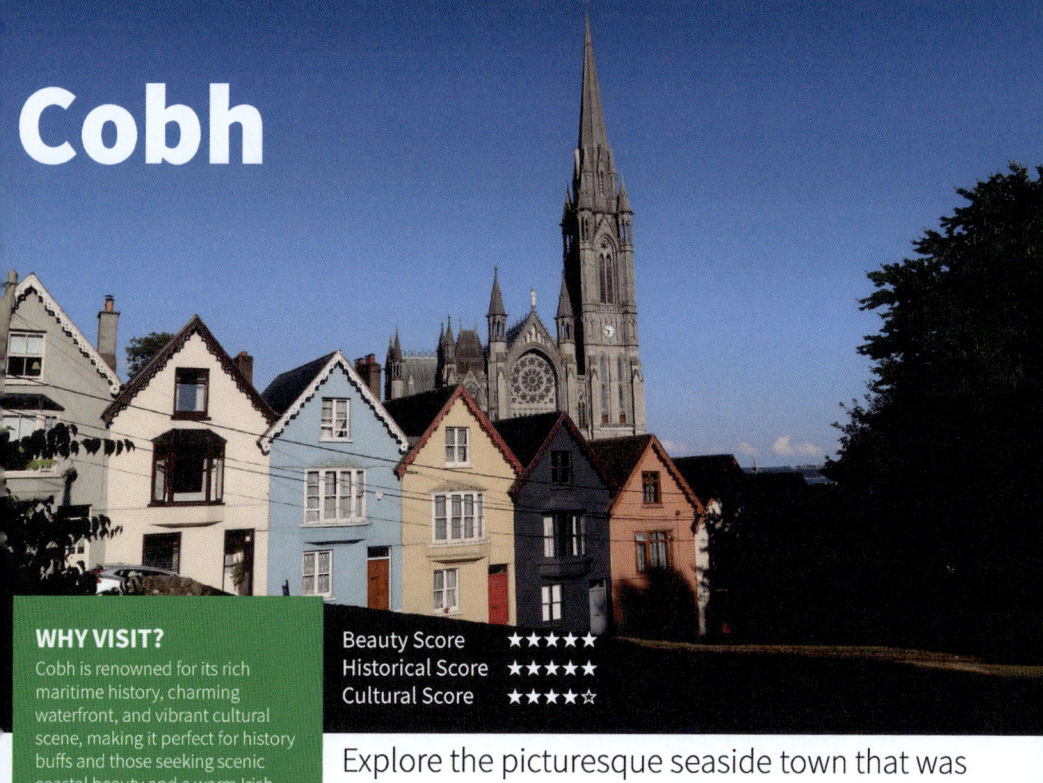

Beauty Score ★★★★★
Historical Score ★★★★★
Cultural Score ★★★★☆

WHY VISIT?
Cobh is renowned for its rich maritime history, charming waterfront, and vibrant cultural scene, making it perfect for history buffs and those seeking scenic coastal beauty and a warm Irish welcome.

FUN FACT!
Cobh's original name, Queenstown, was given following a visit by Queen Victoria in 1849. The name was changed back to Cobh in 1920.

GETTING THERE
Accessible by car and train from Cork city; Cobh is also a popular stop for cruise ships.

County Cork

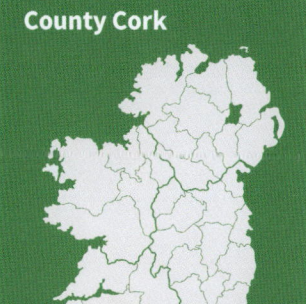

Explore the picturesque seaside town that was the last port of call for the Titanic.

OVERVIEW
Cobh, formerly known as Queenstown, is a charming harbour town on the south coast of County Cork. Recognised as the last port of call for the RMS Titanic on its ill-fated maiden voyage in 1912, Cobh is home to the Titanic Experience. This museum, located inside the original White Star Line ticket office, offers an immersive journey into the history of the ill-fated ocean liner. The town is also home to the Cobh Heritage Centre, which highlights stories of Irish emigration and Cobh's role as a major port. The picturesque St. Colman's Cathedral, perched high above the town, offers stunning views of the harbour. With its colourful houses, bustling promenade, and rich cultural heritage, Cobh is a must-visit destination in County Cork.

BEST TIME TO VISIT
April to September for optimal weather and to enjoy the town's outdoor attractions and events.

TOP FACT
Cobh was the departure point for 2.5 million Irish people who emigrated to North America between 1848 and 1950, many during the Great Famine.

LOCAL LEGEND
Legend speaks of the "Ghost Ship" phenomenon, where phantom vessels are said to appear in the harbour, echoing the town's rich maritime past.

Fota Wildlife Park

Ireland's top wildlife park with roaming animals.

County Cork

OVERVIEW
Fota Wildlife Park is a 100-acre wildlife haven located on Fota Island in County Cork. Established in 1983, the park is home to over 100 animal species, many of which roam freely in open spaces. Visitors have the chance to walk among kangaroos, giraffes, and lemurs while enjoying the natural beauty of the stunning green surroundings. The park is also home to educational exhibits and boasts a strong commitment to conservation, making it both an entertaining and enlightening destination.

WHY VISIT?
Fota Wildlife Park offers an unforgettable wildlife experience in the heart of County Cork. Animals roam freely in carefully designed habitats, making this a must-visit for families, nature enthusiasts, and anyone seeking a unique outdoor adventure in Ireland.

Beauty Score ★★★★☆
Historical Score ★★★☆☆
Cultural Score ★★★★☆

FUN FACT
Fota Wildlife Park is the only place in Ireland where you can see cheetahs up close in their natural habitat.

GETTING THERE
Easily accessible by car, with parking available on site. You can also get the train to Fota station, which is a short walk from the park entrance.

BEST TIME TO VISIT
Spring and summer offer the best weather for outdoor exploration, but the park is enjoyable year-round.

ACCOMMODATION TIPS
Stay at the nearby Fota Island Resort for luxury accommodation just minutes from the park.

Carrauntoohil

Conquer Ireland's highest peak and experience the thrill of standing atop the Kingdom of Kerry.

OVERVIEW
Carrauntoohil is Ireland's tallest mountain, at a formidable 1,038 metres (3,406 ft) in height. The ascent demands physical fitness and appropriate gear, but the reward is unparalleled. This iconic peak is a bucket-list item for many and a testament to Ireland's natural grandeur.

WHY VISIT?
Carrauntoohil, the crown jewel of the MacGillycuddy Reeks, offers a challenging yet rewarding hike for experienced mountaineers. With breathtaking panoramic views of Kerry's stunning landscapes, it's a must-do for any adventure seekers.

BEST TIME TO VISIT
Late Spring to early autumn (May to September) offers the most stable weather conditions for hiking.

Beauty Score ★★★★★
Historical Score ★★★☆☆
Cultural Score ★★★☆☆

County Kerry

FUN FACT!
Carrauntoohil's name translates to 'Tuathal's Sickle', a reference to its distinctive shape.

GETTING THERE:
Accessible from various starting points in the MacGillycuddy Reeks; the Devil's Ladder is a popular hiking route.

Dingle Peninsula

Beauty Score ★★★★★
Historical Score ★★★☆☆
Cultural Score ★★★★★

Experience southwest Ireland's stunning coastal scenery, vibrant culture, and ancient history.

WHY VISIT?

The Dingle Peninsula is renowned for its breathtaking landscapes, charming villages, and rich cultural heritage. Here, you can explore rugged cliffs, sandy beaches, and ancient archaeological sites while enjoying the warm hospitality of the local communities. The peninsula is also famous for its thriving arts scene and traditional Irish music.

FUN FACT!

The Dingle Peninsula was the filming location for scenes in Ryan's Daughter and Star Wars: The Last Jedi.

GETTING THERE

Accessible by car. Dingle Town is approximately a 1.5-hour drive from Tralee and a 2-hour drive from Killarney.

County Kerry

OVERVIEW

The Dingle Peninsula stretches 48 km (30 miles) into the Atlantic Ocean, offering dramatic scenery and a wealth of attractions. Highlights include the town of Dingle, with its colourful harbour and lively pubs, and the Slea Head Drive, a scenic route that offers spectacular coastal views and numerous historical sites, including ancient forts, beehive huts, and early Christian churches. The peninsula is also home to Mount Brandon, one of Ireland's highest peaks, which is excellent for hiking, and plenty of great family activities, like The Dingle Oceanworld Aquarium. Fungie the Dingle Dolphin was Ireland's most loved dolphin who befriended local swimmers and divers for nearly 40 years from the early 1980s. He was well known in this area and disappeared in 2020.

Skellig Michael

Beauty Score ★★★★★
Historical Score ★★★★★
Cultural Score ★★★★★

FUN FACT!
Skellig Michael was featured in several Star Wars films, including The Force Awakens and The Last Jedi, as the location of Luke Skywalker's hermitage.

GETTING THERE
Accessible by boat from Portmagee, County Kerry. Boat trips are weather-dependent and should be booked in advance.

TOP FACT
The monastic settlement on Skellig Michael is one of the best examples of early Christian architecture in Europe, dating back to the 6th century.

County Kerry

Visit a UNESCO World Heritage Site featuring a remote, ancient monastic settlement.

OVERVIEW
Skellig Michael, also known as Great Skellig, is one of Ireland's most iconic and remote attractions. Located 12 km (7.5 miles) off the coast of County Kerry, this steep and rocky island was home to early Christian monks who built a monastery high on its cliffs. The monastery includes beehive huts, stone crosses, and a church, all reached by climbing over 600 steep steps. The island's isolation and dramatic scenery made it an attractive location for the team filming the Star Wars series. Visitors can explore the monastic ruins, enjoy breathtaking views, and observe various seabird species.

WHY VISIT?
Skellig Michael offers a unique and awe-inspiring experience with its rugged beauty, inspiring wildlife, and historical significance. The island is home to a well-preserved 6th-century monastic settlement and provides stunning views of the Atlantic Ocean. It is also a significant wildlife sanctuary, providing a home for seabirds like puffins.

The Ring of Kerry

Experience Ireland's most famous scenic drive.

OVERVIEW
Starting and ending in the town of Killarney, the Ring of Kerry takes you through some of the most beautiful scenery in Ireland. Highlights include Killarney National Park, the Gap of Dunloe, Muckross House, Ladies View, and Torc Waterfall. The route passes through picturesque towns such as Kenmare, Sneem, Waterville, Cahersiveen, and Glenbeigh. Along the way, you can discover ancient stone forts, castles, and monasteries while enjoying outdoor activities such as hiking, cycling, and fishing.

WHY VISIT?
The Ring of Kerry is a spectacular 179 km (111 miles) circular route that showcases some of Ireland's most stunning landscapes. Visitors can enjoy panoramic views of the Atlantic Ocean, rugged coastal stretches, lush rolling hills, and charming Irish towns and villages. The route is also dotted with historical sites, natural wonders, and several cultural attractions, making it a must-visit destination for any traveller to Ireland.

FUN FACT!
The Ring of Kerry is part of the Wild Atlantic Way, a 2,500 km (1,550 mile) coastal route that stretches from Donegal to West Cork.

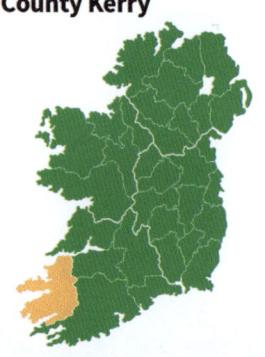

County Kerry

Beauty Score ★★★★★
Historical Score ★★★★★
Cultural Score ★★★★

Ross Castle

Beauty Score ★★★★★
Historical Score ★★★★★
Cultural Score ★★★★☆

FUN FACT!
According to legend, O'Donoghue, the castle's original chieftain, still resides in a deep slumber beneath the waters of Lough Leane. They say he rises every seven years on May Day to circle the lake on his white horse.

GETTING THERE
Easily accessible by car from Killarney Town, with parking near the castle. The site is also accessible by bike or foot via scenic trails from Killarney.

County Kerry

Explore a beautifully restored 15th-century tower house set amongst beautiful surroundings.

OVERVIEW
Built in the late 15th century by the O'Donoghue clan, Ross Castle is a classic example of an Irish tower house. The castle has been meticulously restored and is furnished with 16th and 17th-century oak furniture. Located on the shores of Lough Leane, it provides stunning views and serves as a gateway to Killarney National Park. The castle is open to the public for guided tours, which offer insights into the life and times of its inhabitants. Additionally, boat trips to Innisfallen Island and the Gap of Dunloe are available from the nearby pier.

WHY VISIT?
Ross Castle offers a fascinating glimpse into Ireland's medieval past, with its well-preserved structure and picturesque location amidst the backdrop of Killarney National Park and Lough Leane. Visitors can enjoy guided tours of the castle, learn about its history and significance, and take in the breathtaking scenery of the national park and the surrounding lakes.

BEST TIME TO VISIT
Late Spring to early autumn (May to September) for the best weather and full access to the grounds.

Inch Beach

Enjoy a stunning, expansive beach with breathtaking views of the Atlantic Ocean.

OVERVIEW
Inch Beach is one of the most iconic beaches in Ireland, known for its dramatic beauty and outdoor recreation opportunities. The dune-backed beach offers panoramic views of the Atlantic Ocean, with the mountains of the Dingle Peninsula in the background. It is a popular destination for both locals and tourists, providing a perfect setting for picnics, long walks, and water sports. The beach has been featured in several films, such as Ryan's Daughter and Excalibur.

BEST TIME TO VISIT
Late Spring to early autumn (May to September) for the best weather and water conditions.

GETTING THERE
Easily accessible by car, with parking near the beach. The beach is a short drive from Dingle Town and Killarney.

Beauty Score ★★★★★
Historical Score ★★☆☆☆
Cultural Score ★★★☆☆

WHY VISIT?
Inch Beach is a beautiful, expansive sandy beach stretching 5 km (3 miles) along the Dingle Peninsula. It offers several activities, such as swimming, surfing, windsurfing, and beachcombing. The beach is also a fantastic spot for relaxing and taking in the stunning coastal scenery.

FUN FACT!
Inch Beach is a vast strand extending into Dingle Bay, creating ideal conditions for various water sports.

ACCOMODATION
Stay in nearby Dingle town or in one of the local guest houses or B&Bs in Inch village for easy access to the beach and other attractions on the peninsula.

County Kerry

King John's Castle

Step into a 13th-century castle for an immersive journey through Ireland's medieval history.

OVERVIEW

Built between 1200 and 1210 on the orders of King John of England, this imposing fortress has impressively stood the test of time. Interactive exhibitions bring the castle's history to life, showcasing its construction and siege, as well as the everyday life and daily ongoings that took place within the castle walls. Highlights include the castle's 13th-century towers, its medieval courtyard complete with siege machines, and its visitor centre, which boasts engaging displays and audiovisual presentations. Visitors can also climb the towers to enjoy spectacular views over Limerick City and the River Shannon.

WHY VISIT?

King John's Castle is one of the best-preserved Norman castles in Europe. Providing a captivating visitor experience with its state-of-the-art interpretive centre, medieval courtyard, and panoramic views of the River Shannon, the castle offers a fascinating insight into Limerick's medieval past, making it a must-see for history buffs and families alike.

County Limerick

FUN FACT!
The castle was besieged several times, most notably during the Irish Confederate Wars in the 17th century. Evidence of these sieges can still be seen in the castle walls.

Beauty Score ★★★★☆
Historical Score ★★★★★
Cultural Score ★★★★☆

58

The Rock of Cashel

Discover the iconic Rock of Cashel for medieval architecture and breathtaking views.

WHY VISIT?
The Rock of Cashel is a must-visit for impressive medieval buildings, a rich history that dates back to the 4th century, and a picturesque setting atop a limestone hill.

FUN FACT!
According to legend, the Rock of Cashel originated from a piece of the Devil's Bit Mountain, which St. Patrick had banished in anger.

GETTING THERE
Easily accessible by car, with parking available nearby; also accessible by public transport from nearby towns.

ACCOMMODATION TIPS
Stay in Cashel or nearby towns like Cahir for a range of accommodation options to suit different budgets.

County Tipperary

OVERVIEW
The Rock of Cashel, also known as St. Patrick's Rock, is a prominent archaeological site in the heart of Tipperary. It is one of Ireland's most visited attractions and includes a round tower, cathedral, chapel, and other ecclesiastical buildings spanning a millennium. Originally the seat of the Kings of Munster, it later became a centre of religious power and learning. Today, visitors can explore the site and marvel at its well-preserved architecture while enjoying panoramic views of the surrounding plains from its elevated position.

Beauty Score ★★★★★
Historical Score ★★★★★
Cultural Score ★★★★★

Waterford Greenway

Explore Ireland's longest off-road walking and cycling trail.

GETTING THERE
Accessible from multiple points along the trail, with parking available at Waterford City, Kilmacthomas, and Dungarvan; bikes are available to rent in these towns.

FUN FACT!
The Waterford Greenway follows the route of the old Waterford to Mallow railway line, which was operational from 1878 until it closed in 1982.

TOP FACT
The Greenway features eleven bridges, three viaducts, and one tunnel, each offering unique and scenic viewpoints.

Beauty Score ★★★★★
Historical Score ★★★☆☆
Cultural Score ★★★☆☆

County Waterford

OVERVIEW

The Waterford Greenway, also known as the Déise Greenway, is a converted railway line that stretches 46 km (28.6 miles) from Waterford City to the seaside town of Dungarvan. The trail travels through various landscapes, including lush countryside, coastal scenery, and historic landmarks such as the 200-year-old Durrow Tunnel and the iconic Kilmacthomas Viaduct. The route is mostly flat, making it accessible for all fitness levels, and there are plenty of rest stops, cafes, and picnic areas along the way. The Greenway also offers plenty of opportunities for exploring nearby attractions, such as the Waterford and Suir Valley Railway, Mount Congreve Gardens, and the Copper Coast UNESCO Global Geopark.

WHY VISIT?

The Waterford Greenway offers a beautiful and safe environment for outdoor enthusiasts of all ages and abilities. Whether walking, cycling, or running, guests can discover historical sites, picturesque landscapes, and charming villages along this 46 km (28.6 miles) trail.

LEINSTER

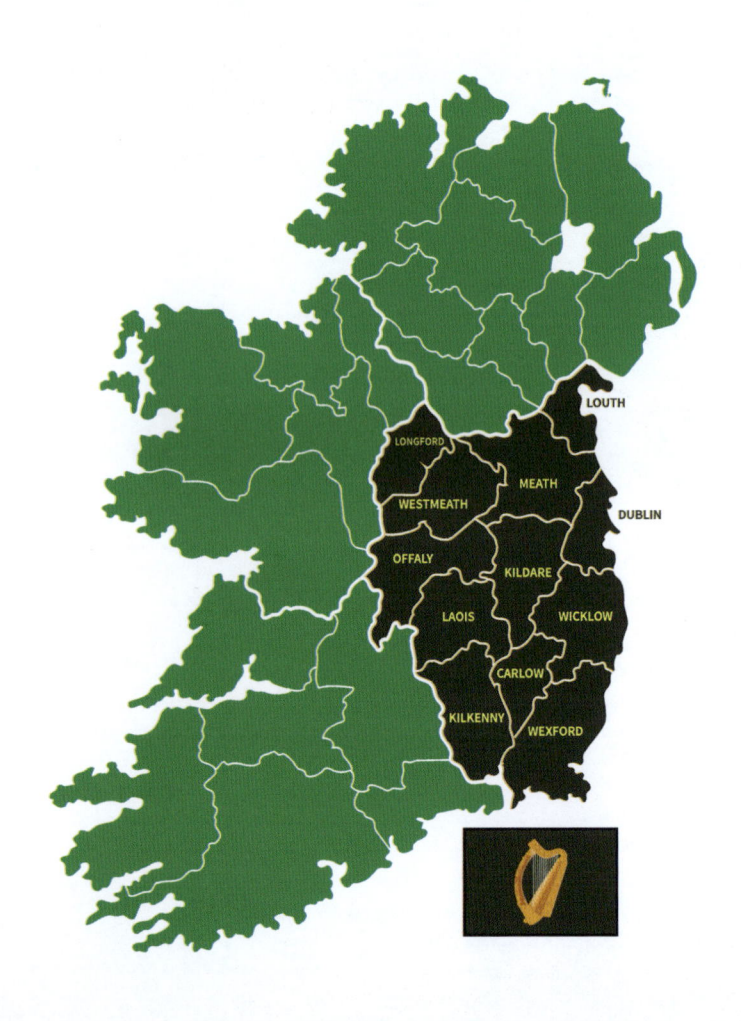

Duckett's Grove

Discover the haunting beauty of a ruined Gothic revival mansion.

OVERVIEW

Located in rural County Carlow countryside, Duckett's Grove was once the home of the influential Duckett family, whose bloodline can be traced back to William the Conqueror and King Edward I. It fell into ruin after a fire in the early 20th century. However, its dramatic Gothic architecture remains a captivating site to this day. Visitors can wander through the shell of the mansion and enjoy the serene gardens, which make it an ideal day out for photographers, history lovers, and explorers. The gardens' beauty and serenity will make you feel relaxed and at peace.

Beauty Score ★★★★☆
Historical Score ★★★★★
Cultural Score ★★★★☆

WHY VISIT?

Duckett's Grove, a striking 19th-century Gothic mansion, offers a unique blend of history and nature. Surrounded by beautiful walled gardens and woodland, its ruins offer a peak into the magnificence of Ireland's aristocratic past. The site is perfect for those seeking history and nature, with walking trails that take you on a journey through the surrounding estate and a garden filled with unique plants and sculptures. The mansion's distinctive features will intrigue and excite history lovers and explorers.

FUN FACT!

The mansion is said to be haunted, with paranormal investigators visiting frequently to uncover the mysteries of the site.

GETTING THERE

A short drive from Carlow town via the R418 road.

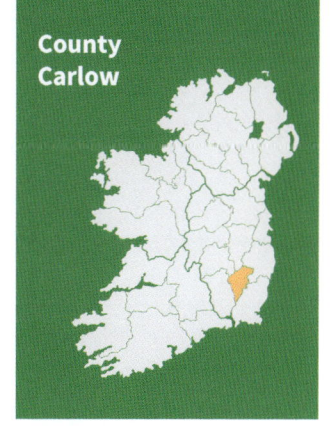

County Carlow

62

Croke Park

County Dublin

Experience the heart of Irish sports and culture at one of Europe's largest and most iconic stadiums.

OVERVIEW
Croke Park, often referred to as 'Croker', is one of the largest stadiums in Europe, with a capacity of 82,300. It serves as the headquarters of the GAA, which governs Gaelic games such as hurling and Gaelic football, the national sports of Ireland. The stadium also features the GAA Museum, where you can learn the extensive history of Gaelic games and the stadium itself through exhibits and interactive displays. Visitors can take guided tours of the stadium, offering a behind-the-scenes look at the dressing rooms and VIP areas, as well as a chance to walk in the footsteps of legends on the pitch. With its modern facilities and historical significance, Croke Park is an iconic symbol of Irish sporting life.

Beauty Score ★★★★☆
Historical Score ★★★★★
Cultural Score ★★★★★

WHY VISIT?
Croke Park is the main headquarters and stadium of the Gaelic Athletic Association (GAA), making it a must-visit for sports enthusiasts and those interested in Irish sporting culture. The stadium hosts major Gaelic football and hurling matches, as well as concerts and events, offering a vibrant atmosphere and a solid connection to Irish lifestyle and heritage.

FUN FACT!
Croke Park has a unique skywalk tour, the Etihad Skyline, which offers panoramic views of Dublin from the stadium's roof.

GETTING THERE
Easily accessible by public transport, with the Drumcondra train station and several bus routes nearby. Parking is also available for visitors.

Glasnevin Cemetery

Discover Ireland's largest cemetery, the final resting place of many notable figures.

OVERVIEW
Established in 1832, Glasnevin Cemetery spans 124 acres and contains over 1.5 million burials. The cemetery is known for its beautiful Victorian garden design, historical monuments, and the iconic O'Connell Tower, which offers panoramic views of Dublin. Visitors can take guided tours to learn about the notable figures buried here, such as Daniel O'Connell, Michael Collins, and Countess Markievicz. The Glasnevin Museum enhances the experience with interactive exhibits and a genealogical research centre.

WHY VISIT?
Glasnevin Cemetery is a unique and fascinating destination, offering insight into Ireland's history through the stories of those buried here. It is the final resting place of many prominent Irish figures, including political leaders, writers, and revolutionaries. The cemetery also features the Glasnevin Museum, which includes detailed exhibitions about the history of the cemetery and the lives of the people interred there.

LOCAL LEGEND
Grave robbers once plagued the cemetery in the 19th century, leading to the construction of watchtowers to deter them.

Beauty Score ★★★☆☆
Historical Score ★★★★★
Cultural Score ★★★★☆

FUN FACT!
Glasnevin Cemetery is home to the tallest round tower in Ireland, the O'Connell Tower, standing at 55 metres (180 feet).

ACCOMODATION
Easily accessible by bus from Dublin city centre. The cemetery is also a short distance from Dublin's Botanic Gardens, making it easy to visit both attractions in one go.

County Dublin

Kilmainham Gaol

Step into one of Ireland's most significant historical sites, where many leaders of Irish rebellions were imprisoned and executed.

OVERVIEW

Opened in 1796 and operating for 128 years, Kilmainham Gaol was a notorious Irish prison that held thousands of men, women, and children. It is most famous for being the location where many leaders of the 1916 Easter Rising were incarcerated – many of them were later executed in the prison's yard. The gaol was decommissioned in 1924 and later restored as a museum. Today, it stands as a powerful symbol of Ireland's turbulent history, with guided tours that provide detailed accounts of the lives of the prisoners and the central role of the gaol in Irish history.

WHY VISIT?

Kilmainham Gaol offers a sobering yet fascinating insight into Ireland's struggle for independence. The gaol has housed many notable figures from throughout Irish history and played a vital role in the events leading up to the establishment of the Irish Republic. Visitors can explore the cells, learn about the harsh conditions, and understand the impact of the prison on Ireland's fight for freedom.

FUN FACT!
Kilmainham Gaol's East Wing has been featured in numerous films, including In the Name of the Father and The Italian Job.

GETTING THERE
Easily accessible by public transport, including bus and Luas (tram), with parking available nearby.

BEST TIME TO VISIT
Year-round, with indoor exhibits making it suitable for any weather.

Beauty Score ★★★☆☆
Historical Score ★★★★★
Cultural Score ★★★★★

County Dublin

Temple Bar

Experience Dublin's vibrant night-life in the heart of the city, known for its lively pubs, street performers, and cultural attractions.

WHY VISIT?
Temple Bar is Dublin's cultural quarter and a hotspot for night-life. It offers an array of pubs, bars, and restaurants, along with live music, art galleries, and theatres. Whether you're looking for traditional Irish music, contemporary art, or a bustling atmosphere, Temple Bar has something for everyone.

Beauty Score ★★★★☆
Historical Score ★★★★☆
Cultural Score ★★★★★

FUN FACT!
Despite its modern reputation, Temple Bar was historically a marshy area reclaimed from the river in the 17th century, and its name is believed to have originated from Sir William Temple, who owned property there.

TOP FACT
The Temple Bar Pub, one of the most iconic spots in the area, dates back to 1840 and is famous for its extensive whiskey collection and live traditional music.

County Dublin

OVERVIEW
Temple Bar is a cobblestone area on the south bank of the River Liffey, known for its preserved medieval street pattern and vibrant atmosphere. It is home to some of Dublin's most famous pubs, such as The Temple Bar Pub and The Porterhouse. The area is also rich in cultural institutions, including the Irish Film Institute, Temple Bar Gallery and Studios, and the Button Factory. A night out here offers a blend of traditional and modern Irish experiences, with something to cater to every taste.

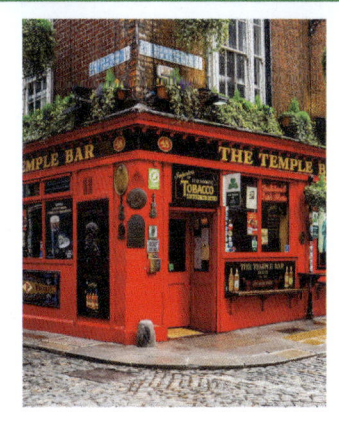

LOCAL LEGEND
The area is known for its street performers and buskers, who have become an integral part of its vibrant night-life, adding to the area's charm and allure.

The Brazen Head

Enjoy a pint at Dublin's oldest pub, offering a lively atmosphere, traditional music, and hearty food.

OVERVIEW

The Brazen Head has served patrons for over 800 years, making it a significant landmark in Dublin's history. The pub's interior retains much of its historic charm with low ceilings, wooden beams, and cosy nooks. Visitors can enjoy live traditional Irish music sessions every night and storytelling evenings that provide a glimpse into Ireland's folklore and literary heritage. The menu features classic Irish dishes, such as beef and Guinness stew, alongside a wide selection of beers, whiskeys, and spirits.

WHY VISIT?

The Brazen Head is Dublin's oldest pub, dating back to 1198. It offers a unique combination of historical charm, vibrant atmosphere, and traditional Irish music. The pub's rich history and character make it a must-visit for anyone looking for an authentic Irish pub experience.

FUN FACT!

The Brazen Head has hosted many famous figures throughout its history, including literary greats like James Joyce and Jonathan Swift and revolutionary leaders like Michael Collins and Robert Emmet.

Beauty Score	★★★☆☆
Historical Score	★★★★★
Cultural Score	★★★★★

GETTING THERE

Easily accessible by public transport, including bus and Luas (tram), and a short walk from Christchurch Cathedral and Temple Bar.

County Dublin

The General Post Office (GPO)

Visit the iconic site of the 1916 Easter Rising, a symbol of Irish independence and history.

OVERVIEW
Completed in 1818, the GPO is a grand Georgian building located on Dublin's main thoroughfare, O'Connell Street. It was the headquarters of the Irish Volunteers during the 1916 Easter Rising, a pivotal event in Ireland's fight for independence. Today, the building is home to an informative museum, GPO Witness History, which provides interactive exhibits on the Easter Rising, the War of Independence, and the broader history of the Irish postal service. Visitors can explore the historic main hall, with its iconic columns and high ceilings, and learn about some of the most significant events that shaped modern Ireland.

TOP FACT
The GPO still functions as a post office today, making it one of the oldest working post offices in the world.

GETTING THERE
Easily accessible by public transport, including bus, Luas (tram), and DART (Dublin Area Rapid Transit), with stops near O'Connell Street.

Beauty Score ★★★★☆
Historical Score ★★★★★
Cultural Score ★★★★☆

WHY VISIT?
The General Post Office is one of Dublin's most historically significant buildings, playing a central role in the 1916 Easter Rising. It offers a chance to learn about Ireland's struggle for independence and to view a beautifully preserved piece of Georgian architecture.

FUN FACT!
The statue of Irish mythological hero Cúchulainn, located within the GPO, commemorates those who died in the 1916 Easter Rising.

County Dublin

The Guinness Storehouse

WHY VISIT?
The Guinness Storehouse offers an immersive experience into the world of Guinness, highlighting its rich history and brewing process through interactive exhibits and tastings. It's a must-visit for beer enthusiasts and those interested in Irish heritage.

FUN FACT!
The 9,000-year lease signed by Arthur Guinness for the St. James's Gate Brewery in 1759 is still in effect today.

GETTING THERE
Easily accessible by public transport, with nearby bus and Luas (tram) stops; ample parking is also available nearby.

County Dublin

Discover the history of Ireland's most iconic beer at the Guinness Storehouse, where brewing tradition meets modern innovation.

OVERVIEW
The Guinness Storehouse, located at the historic St. James's Gate Brewery, is Dublin's top tourist attraction. Spanning seven floors, the Storehouse guides visitors through the story of the famous stout, from its origins in 1759 to its global success today. Highlights include an overview of the brewing process, Guinness' iconic advertising history, and the Gravity Bar, where visitors can enjoy a perfectly poured pint of Guinness while soaking up panoramic views of Dublin. Interactive exhibits and tastings make this an engaging and educational experience for all ages.

BEST TIME TO VISIT
Year-round, with fewer crowds during weekday mornings.

TOP FACT
The Gravity Bar, located on the top floor, offers 360-degree views of Dublin and is the highest bar in the city.

LOCAL LEGEND
It is said that Arthur Guinness's decision to sign a 9,000-year lease was driven by a deep belief in the future success of his beer, which has indeed become iconic worldwide.

Beauty Score ★★★★☆
Historical Score ★★★★★
Cultural Score ★★★★★

Irish Emigration Museum

Discover the compelling stories of Irish emigration and the global influence of the Irish diaspora.

OVERVIEW

Located in the historic CHQ Building in Dublin's Docklands, the Irish Emigration Museum (EPIC) is an award-winning museum dedicated to the history and impact of Irish emigration. With over 20 interactive galleries, visitors can discover the myriad reasons why people left Ireland, the challenges they faced, and how they influenced the wider world. Highlights include digital storytelling, personal testimonies, and a range of multimedia displays that bring to life the experiences of the ten million people who have emigrated from Ireland over the centuries.

WHY VISIT?

EPIC The Irish Emigration Museum provides a comprehensive and engaging look at the history of Irish emigration. Interactive exhibits and immersive experiences detail the personal stories and cultural contributions of Irish emigrants worldwide. This state-of-the-art museum offers a unique and emotional journey through stories of Ireland's diaspora.

Beauty Score ★★★★☆
Historical Score ★★★★☆
Cultural Score ★★★★★

FUN FACT!
EPIC was named Europe's Leading Tourist Attraction at the World Travel Awards in 2019 and 2020.

GETTING THERE
Easily accessible by public transport, with nearby bus, tram (Luas), and train stations. Parking is also available at the CHQ Building.

County Dublin

John Kavanagh

Famous for the best pint of Guinness in Dublin, maybe Ireland.

OVERVIEW
Established in 1833, John Kavanagh - The Gravediggers is a timeless gem of Irish pub culture. Situated next to Glasnevin Cemetery, the pub got its nickname because gravediggers would stop in after a hard day's work. Its unspoiled interior, lack of music or televisions, and perfectly poured Guinness have earned it legendary status among both locals and visitors. The pub is often cited as the home of Dublin's best pint, making it a pilgrimage site for beer enthusiasts.

WHY VISIT?
Renowned for serving what many call the best pint of Guinness in Ireland, John Kavanagh's is a haven of tradition and charm. Its historic setting and unique atmosphere make it an essential stop for lovers of Irish culture and a good pint.

FUN FACT!
The Guinness at The Gravediggers is said to be so fresh and perfectly poured that it's considered a benchmark for the iconic drink.

GETTING THERE
Conveniently reached by bus or taxi; a short walk from Glasnevin Cemetery.

County Dublin

Beauty Score ★★★☆☆
Historical Score ★★★★★
Cultural Score ★★★★★

Trinity College

Beauty Score ★★★★★
Historical Score ★★★★★
Cultural Score ★★★★★

Explore Ireland's oldest and most prestigious university.

OVERVIEW

Founded in 1592, Trinity College Dublin is Ireland's leading university and a prominent landmark in the capital city. The campus boasts beautiful historic buildings, cobblestone paths, and lush green spaces. The Old Library, a highlight of any visit, houses the historic Book of Kells, an illuminated manuscript created by Celtic monks around the 9th century. The Long Room, a stunning library hall within the Old Library, contains over 200,000 of Trinity's oldest books. The university also features several museums, including the Science Gallery and the Douglas Hyde Gallery, making it a hub of learning and culture.

WHY VISIT?

Trinity College Dublin offers a rich blend of history, culture, and academic excellence. Visitors can marvel at the magnificent Old Library, view the Book of Kells, and stroll through the picturesque campus grounds that have inspired scholars for centuries.

FUN FACT!

The Book of Kells was written around 800 AD and is considered one of the finest examples of a medieval illuminated manuscript.

GETTING THERE

Easily accessible by public transport, with nearby bus, tram (Luas), and train stations; parking is limited in the city centre.

County Dublin

72

St. Stephen's Green

Relax in one of Dublin's most iconic and beautiful public parks, surrounded by vibrant city life.

OVERVIEW
Established in 1664, St. Stephen's Green is a historical city park that spans 22 acres in the heart of Dublin. It includes a mix of Victorian landscaping with flower beds, statues, and a central lake with a waterfall and bridge. The park is bordered by important landmarks such as the Royal College of Surgeons and the Shelbourne Hotel. Visitors can explore various monuments, including the Fusilier's Arch, dedicated to the Royal Dublin Fusiliers who fought in the Second Boer War, and a statue of the Irish poet W.B. Yeats.

WHY VISIT?
St. Stephen's Green offers a serene escape in the heart of Dublin, with beautifully landscaped gardens, historical monuments, and a picturesque lake. The park is perfect for a leisurely stroll, a picnic, or to unwind amidst nature.

FUN FACT!
During the 1916 Easter Rising, a temporary ceasefire was called to allow park groundsmen to feed the ducks in St. Stephen's Green.

County Dublin

Beauty Score ★★★★★
Historical Score ★★★★☆
Cultural Score ★★★☆☆

GETTING THERE
Easily accessible by public transport, including bus, Luas (tram), and a short walk from Grafton Street.

Dublin Castle

Explore the historic heart of Dublin with a blend of medieval, Georgian, and modern architecture.

OVERVIEW

Dublin Castle has been central to Irish history for centuries. Built in the early 13th century on the site of a Viking settlement, the castle served as the seat of British administration in Ireland until 1922. Today, visitors can explore the State Apartments, Medieval Undercroft, and Chapel Royal. Meanwhile, the gardens and courtyard provide a tranquil escape in the heart of the city. Dublin Castle also hosts various cultural events and exhibitions throughout the year.

WHY VISIT?

Dublin Castle is a must-visit landmark that offers a deep dive into Ireland's history, from its origins as a Viking fortress to its role in British rule and its current function as a central government complex. The castle features beautiful gardens, historical exhibitions, and the State Apartments used for state functions.

Beauty Score ★★★★☆
Historical Score ★★★★★
Cultural Score ★★★★☆

County Dublin

FUN FACT!

The Record Tower is the only remaining part of the original medieval castle, dating back to the 13th century.

GETTING THERE

Easily accessible by public transport, including bus, Luas (tram), and DART (Dublin Area Rapid Transit).

Castletown House

Ireland's largest and grandest Palladian mansion.

County Kildare

FUN FACT!
Castletown House is the first and largest Palladian-style house built in Ireland, setting a standard for Georgian architecture in the country.

GETTING THERE
A short drive from Dublin via the N4 motorway or accessible by bus.

TRAVEL TIP
Take a leisurely walk around the Long Gallery and don't miss the serene river walks on the grounds.

OVERVIEW

Located in Celbridge, County Kildare, Castletown House was first built in 1722 for William Conolly, former Speaker of the Irish House of Commons. Regarded as one of the finest examples of Palladian architecture in Ireland, visitors can explore the beautifully decorated rooms and extensive gardens, with many areas now open to the public after careful restoration. The grounds also feature several scenic walking trails and a café for visitors and families to enjoy a fantastic day out.

WHY VISIT?

Castletown House offers a remarkable glimpse into 18th-century aristocratic life in Ireland. A masterpiece of Palladian architecture, this grand mansion features beautifully restored interiors, impressive art collections, and stunning parklands. Book onto a guided tour to gain rich historical insights, which make this spot a must-visit for history buffs and architecture lovers alike.

Beauty Score ★★★★☆
Historical Score ★★★★★
Cultural Score ★★★☆☆

75

Kilkenny Castle

Explore the meticulously restored 12th-century Kilkenny Castle.

OVERVIEW
Built in 1195 by William Marshal, 1st Earl of Pembroke, Kilkenny Castle has played a pivotal role in Ireland's history. As the principal seat of the Butler family for almost 600 years before being sold to the people of Kilkenny in 1967 for £50, the castle boasts strong links to Ireland's rich cultural history and heritage. Today, it is a significant tourist attraction, featuring grand rooms furnished with period pieces, an art gallery, and extensive grounds that are perfect for leisurely walks. Highlights include the Long Gallery, the Drawing Room, and the castle's beautifully landscaped gardens.

WHY VISIT?
Kilkenny Castle is one of Ireland's most iconic and well-preserved castles. It blends medieval architecture and Victorian grandeur, surrounded by beautiful gardens and parkland. The castle is a must-visit for history enthusiasts, families, and anyone interested in Ireland's cultural heritage.

FUN FACT!
The castle has a unique architectural style reflecting various periods, including the medieval, Tudor, and Victorian eras.

GETTING THERE
Easily accessible by car, bus, or train from Dublin, with nearby parking.

BEST TIME TO VISIT
Year-round, with spring and summer (April to September) offering the best weather for exploring the gardens and grounds.

Beauty Score ★★★★★
Historical Score ★★★★★
Cultural Score ★★★★☆

County Kilkenny

Rock of Dunamase

Marvel at the ruins of a medieval stronghold atop a limestone hill.

OVERVIEW
Perched on a rocky outcrop in County Laois, the Rock of Dunamase has been fortified since the early Christian period. The current ruins date to the 12th century when it acted as a critical Anglo-Norman stronghold. Today, visitors can wander through the remains of the castle walls and enjoy panoramic views of the surrounding landscape, embarking on a journey through Irish history and legends at this atmospheric spot.

WHY VISIT?
The Rock of Dunamase is a dramatic historical site home to the remains of a medieval Irish castle. Offering breathtaking views of the surrounding countryside, the site has a storied past and played a significant role as a strategic fortress throughout Ireland's history. Perfect for history lovers and photographers, this ancient ruin invites exploration and reflection.

County Laois

GETTING THERE
A short drive from Portlaoise via the N80 road.

BEST TIME TO VISIT
Spring and summer for the best weather and clear views of the countryside.

FUN FACT!
The Rock of Dunamase was once part of the dowry for Aoife, the daughter of Diarmait Mac Murchada, who married the Norman lord Strongbow in 1170.

Beauty Score ★★★★★
Historical Score ★★★★☆
Cultural Score ★★★☆☆

Lough Ree

Explore Ireland's second-largest lake, steeped in history and nature.

OVERVIEW
Lough Ree, often referred to as the "Lake of Kings," spans Counties Longford, Westmeath, and Roscommon. As one of the largest lakes in Ireland, it boasts a rich history, from ancient monastic settlements to Viking invasions. Visitors can explore its many islands, such as Inchcleraun, which features fascinating ruins of early Christian churches. The lake is a haven for wildlife, including otters, herons, and trout, and provides an idyllic setting for leisurely cruises or adventurous kayaking trips. Its scenic beauty and peaceful atmosphere make it a must-visit for anyone traveling through the midlands.

WHY VISIT?
Lough Ree offers a stunning blend of tranquil waters, lush islands, and diverse wildlife, making it a perfect destination for nature lovers, fishing enthusiasts, and history buffs. Its central location on the River Shannon makes it easily accessible and ideal for boating and water sports.

FUN FACT
Lough Ree is home to "The Dead Centre of Ireland," a point on the lake's eastern shore marking Ireland's geographical centre.

County Longford

Beauty Score ★★★★☆
Historical Score ★★★☆☆
Cultural Score ★★★☆☆

GETTING THERE
Accessible by car via the N63 or N55, with boat tours departing from Athlone.

Proleek Dolmen

Discover one of Ireland's finest and most impressive megalithic monuments.

OVERVIEW
Proleek Dolmen, also known as the Giant's Load, dates back to around 3000 BCE. Consisting of three upright stones that support a large, flat capstone estimated to weigh around 40 tons, the Dolmen is a truly unique historical attraction. You can also view the nearby wedge tomb, which adds to the sight's archaeological significance. Located on the grounds of the Ballymascanlon House Hotel, the Dolmen is easily accessible to visitors, and the surrounding area offers beautiful landscapes and views of the Cooley Mountains, making it an ideal spot for a leisurely walk and exploration of Ireland's ancient history.

BEST TIME TO VISIT
Year-round, with spring and summer (April to September) offering the best weather for outdoor exploration.

GETTING THERE
Accessible by car, with parking available at Ballymascanlon House Hotel. The Dolmen is a short walk from the hotel grounds.

Beauty Score ★★★★☆
Historical Score ★★★★★
Cultural Score ★★★★☆

WHY VISIT?
Proleek Dolmen is a striking example of a Neolithic portal tomb featuring a massive capstone balanced on slender upright stones. This ancient monument is set against the scenic backdrop of the Cooley Peninsula and offers a fascinating glimpse into Ireland's prehistoric past.

FUN FACT!
According to local legend, the Dolmen was created by a giant who carried the enormous capstone from Scotland to Ireland. It is also said that you will be blessed with good luck if you can throw a pebble onto the capstone and it stays.

County Louth

St Peter's Church

Visit one of Ireland's most historic churches, home to the preserved head of St. Oliver Plunkett.

OVERVIEW

Located in the town of Drogheda, St Peter's Church is a prime example of Gothic Revival architecture. Built in the 19th century, the church is renowned for its beautiful facade, intricate stained glass windows, and elaborate interior design. What sets this church apart, however, is that it is home to the preserved head of St. Oliver Plunkett, the martyred Archbishop of Armagh who was canonised in 1975. Visitors can view the relic in a dedicated shrine and learn about St. Oliver Plunkett's life and martyrdom through informative displays. The church remains an active place of worship and a key cultural landmark in the centre of Drogheda.

WHY VISIT?

St Peter's Church is a beautiful and historically significant Catholic church known for its Gothic Revival architecture, exquisite interior, and the relic of St. Oliver Plunkett. It's a popular pilgrimage site and a fascinating destination for those interested in Ireland's religious history.

County Louth

FUN FACT!

St Peter's Church houses the largest set of stained glass windows in all of Ireland, created by the renowned Munich artist Franz Mayer.

Beauty Score	★★★☆☆
Historical Score	★★★★★
Cultural Score	★★★★☆

Carlingford Lough

Discover the natural beauty and tranquillity of a picturesque fjord surrounded by mountains.

OVERVIEW

Carlingford Lough is a glacial fjord that stretches between the Cooley Peninsula in County Louth and the Mourne Mountains in County Down. Renowned for its breathtaking scenery, diverse array of wildlife, and fascinating historical significance, the Lough is a must-visit while exploring the area. The charming village of Carlingford, located on the Lough's southern shore, is known for its medieval heritage, with attractions such as King John's Castle and Taaffe's Castle. The area is also famous for its oysters, and visitors can indulge in fresh seafood from renowned local restaurants. Carlingford Lough is ideal for a day trip or a weekend getaway, offering activities like kayaking, hiking the Cooley Mountains, and exploring the Carlingford-Omeath Greenway.

County Louth

Beauty Score ★★★★★
Historical Score ★★★★☆
Cultural Score ★★★★☆

WHY VISIT?

Carlingford Lough is a stunning natural attraction that provides a perfect blend of scenic beauty, outdoor adventure, and an insight into Ireland's rich history. While here, you can indulge in hiking, sailing, and exploring medieval sights while also taking in breathtaking views of the Mourne and Cooley Mountains.

FUN FACT!

Carlingford Lough is one of only three glacial fjords in Ireland.

GETTING THERE

Easily accessible by car from Dublin (about 90 minutes) and Belfast (about 75 minutes). Free and paid parking is available in Carlingford Village.

Hill of Tara

Beauty Score ★★★★☆
Historical Score ★★★★★
Cultural Score ★★★★★

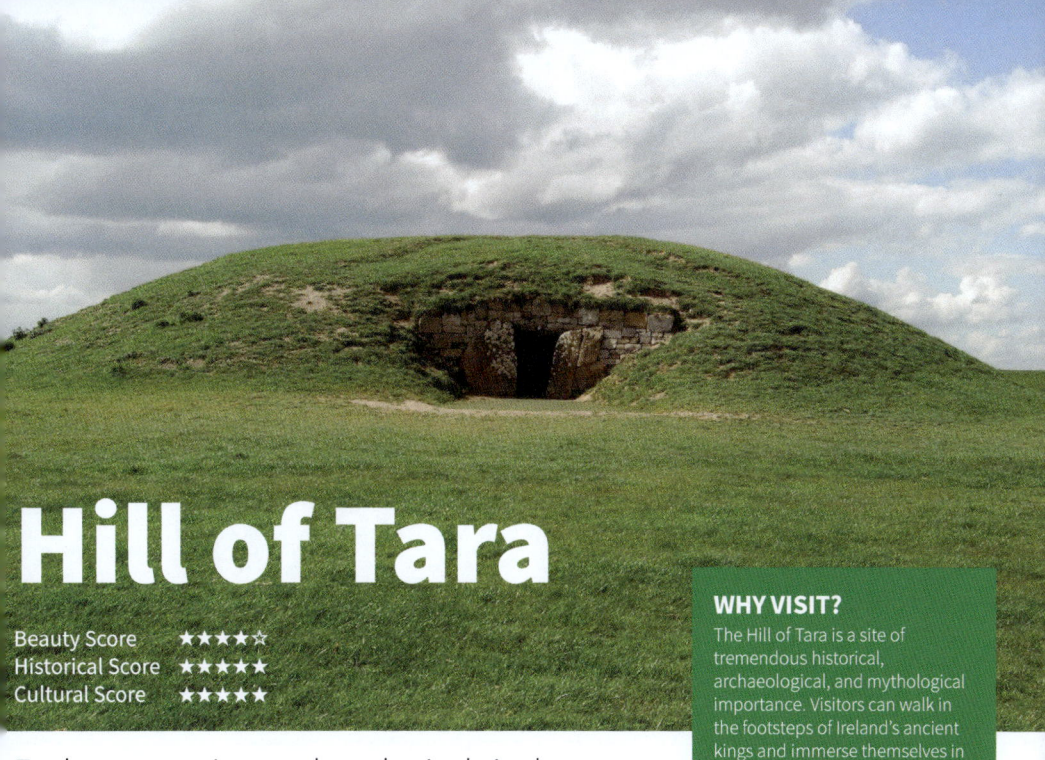

Explore an ancient archaeological site known as the seat of the High Kings of Ireland.

OVERVIEW

The Hill of Tara in County Meath is a significant archaeological site once the political and spiritual centre of ancient Ireland. The site includes several ancient monuments and earthworks, such as the Mound of the Hostages, the Stone of Destiny (Lia Fáil), and the Royal Enclosure. Legend states that it was here that the High Kings of Ireland were inaugurated, making it a significant site in Irish folklore. The Hill of Tara offers stunning views of the surrounding countryside, making it a beautiful spot for walks and reflection. Guided tours are also available, which provide historical insights and detailed explanations of the site's significance.

WHY VISIT?

The Hill of Tara is a site of tremendous historical, archaeological, and mythological importance. Visitors can walk in the footsteps of Ireland's ancient kings and immerse themselves in the island's rich heritage. The perfect destination for history buffs and mythology enthusiasts, it allows visitors to truly discover a deep connection to Ireland's past.

FUN FACT!

The Stone of Destiny, or Lia Fáil, is believed to roar when touched by the rightful king of Ireland.

GETTING THERE

Accessible by car, with parking available near the site. Also reachable by bus from Dublin to Navan, followed by a short taxi ride.

County Meath

Newgrange

Experience one of the world's oldest and most iconic prehistoric sites.

OVERVIEW
Newgrange is a prehistoric monument built around 3200 BC, making it older than Stonehenge and the Great Pyramids of Giza. This sizeable circular mound is part of the Brú na Bóinne complex, with its central feature being an impressive passage tomb. The tomb aligns with the rising sun during the winter solstice, which leads to a magical illumination of the inner chamber as it lets in a thin shaft of sunlight. The site also includes intricate carvings and megalithic art, showcasing its prehistoric builders' advanced skills. Visitors can explore the monument through guided tours that provide insights into its construction, purpose, and the people who built it. The nearby Brú na Bóinne Visitor Centre offers additional exhibits and information about the site and its historical context.

WHY VISIT?
Newgrange is a UNESCO World Heritage site and one of Europe's most significant Neolithic monuments. Its architectural brilliance, astronomical alignment, and historical importance make it a bucket list-worthy destination for anyone interested in ancient history, archaeology, and Irish heritage.

County Meath

GETTING THERE:
Newgrange is accessible by car with parking at the Brú na Bóinne Visitor Centre. The site is also reachable by bus from Dublin to Drogheda, followed by a local bus or taxi to the Visitor Centre.

FUN FACT!
Every year, a few people are selected by lottery to witness the winter solstice illumination from inside the tomb.

Beauty Score ★★★★★
Historical Score ★★★★★
Cultural Score ★★★★★

Trim Castle

Beauty Score ★★★★★
Historical Score ★★★★★
Cultural Score ★★★★☆

Explore the largest Anglo-Norman castle in Ireland.

WHY VISIT?
Trim Castle is a magnificent and well-preserved example of medieval architecture, offering visitors a glimpse into Ireland's turbulent history. With an impressive structure and picturesque location along the River Boyne, Trim Castle is a fascinating destination for history enthusiasts and tourists alike.

GETTING THERE
Accessible by car with parking available nearby; also reachable by bus from Dublin and other nearby towns.

FUN FACT!
Trim Castle was a major filming location in the 1995 movie Braveheart, starring Mel Gibson.

County Meath

OVERVIEW

Trim Castle was constructed in the late 12th century and is the largest and one of the best-preserved Anglo-Norman castles in Ireland. The castle was built by Hugh de Lacy and his son Walter and played a significant role during the Norman conquest of Ireland. The massive three-story keep, which dominates the site, was designed to be both a fortress and a residence. Visitors can explore the castle's extensive grounds, towers, and the keep itself, where guided tours provide fascinating insights into its construction, history, and the lives of its inhabitants. The historical significance of the castle is complemented by its scenic setting on the banks of the River Boyne, from where you can enjoy beautiful views and photographic opportunities.

BEST TIME TO VISIT

Late Spring to early autumn (April to September) for the best weather and full access to the castle grounds.

84

Birr Castle Demesne

Beauty Score ★★★★★
Historical Score ★★★★★
Cultural Score ★★★★☆

FUN FACT!
The Great Telescope, also known as the Leviathan of Parsonstown, was the largest in the world from 1845 until 1917 and was used to discover the spiral nature of galaxies.

GETTING THERE
The estate is accessible by car, with parking available on-site. It is also reachable by bus from nearby towns such as Tullamore.

BEST TIME TO VISIT
Late Spring to early autumn (April to September) for the best weather and to see the gardens in full bloom.

County Offaly

Explore one of Ireland's most beautiful estates and visit the famous Great Telescope.

OVERVIEW
Birr Castle Demesne is located in the heart of Ireland. It is a magnificent estate known for its stunning gardens, historic castle, and pioneering scientific achievements. The castle has been the seat of the Parsons family, the Earls of Rosse, for over four centuries. The demesne features beautifully landscaped gardens, including the formal gardens, the Great Victorian Fernery, and the lake with its tranquil surroundings, making this the perfect place to explore on a sunny afternoon. One of the estate's most notable attractions is the Great Telescope, which was built in the 1840s by the Third Earl of Rosse. Guests can also explore the Science Centre, which highlights the contributions of the Parsons family to astronomy and engineering.

WHY VISIT?
Birr Castle Demesne offers a unique blend of historical significance, scientific heritage, and natural beauty. It's perfect for families, history enthusiasts, and nature lovers keen to enjoy a day out at one of Ireland's most enchanting estates.

Leap Castle

Discover the chilling history of Ireland's most haunted castle.

OVERVIEW
Built in the late 15th century by the O'Carroll clan, Leap Castle is infamous for its violent history and various hauntings. The castle's past is marked by betrayal, murder, and intrigue – you must visit the infamous 'Bloody Chapel', where many brutal events occurred. Today, Leap Castle is privately owned but open to visitors, offering guided tours that delve into its dark history and paranormal activity. The current owner, Sean Ryan, often shares personal stories of his ghostly encounters, adding to the castle's eerie reputation.

WHY VISIT?
With its bloodstained history, Leap Castle brings you on a journey to to explore one of Ireland's most haunted sites. Along the way, you can also learn about the castle's ghostly legends. Visitors can tour the castle, learn about its bloody history, and potentially encounter its famous spirits.

BEST TIME TO VISIT
Anytime, though night tours are particularly popular for those interested in its paranormal aspect.

LOCAL LEGEND
The castle's "Elemental" spirit is said to be a dark, shadowy figure with a foul smell, believed to have been summoned by the Druids or created by the violence of the castle's history.

County Offaly

Beauty Score ★★★★☆
Historical Score ★★★★☆
Cultural Score ★★★★★

GETTING THERE
Accessible by car, with parking available at the castle.

FUN FACT!
Leap Castle is said to be haunted by several spirits, including the Red Lady, a tall spectral figure clad in a red gown who is often seen carrying a dagger.

Sean's Bar

Visit the oldest pub in Ireland, which is one of the oldest in the world.

OVERVIEW
Sean's Bar is located in the heart of Athlone on the banks of the River Shannon. Currently, it holds the Guinness World Record for being the oldest pub in Ireland with its origins traced as far back as AD 900. The bar has a rich history reflected in its ancient walls and memorabilia and has maintained its traditional charm with its old-style decor, cosy atmosphere, and inviting fireplace. Live music sessions, friendly staff, and a wide selection of drinks make it an excellent spot for both locals and tourists.

WHY VISIT?
Sean's Bar uniquely blends history, culture, and Irish hospitality. Visitors can enjoy a pint in a pub that dates back to AD 900, making it a unique spot for history enthusiasts and those looking to experience authentic Irish pub culture.

FUN FACT
During renovations, ancient wattle, daub walls, and old coins were discovered, further confirming the pub's ancient origins.

County Westmeath

Beauty Score ★★★☆☆
Historical Score ★★★★★
Cultural Score ★★★★★

GETTING THERE
Easily accessible by car, with parking available nearby. You can also reach by public transport with bus and train services to and from Athlone.

87

Glendalough

Explore a stunning glacial valley, home to one of Ireland's most important monastic sites.

OVERVIEW

Glendalough, meaning 'Valley of the Two Lakes', is a picturesque valley in the heart of the Wicklow Mountains. This area is rich in history, with ruins of a monastic settlement that was founded by St. Kevin in the 6th century, including a remarkable round tower, several churches, and a cathedral. It also boasts stunning natural beauty, with two beautiful lakes surrounded by wooded hills and rugged mountains. Visitors can explore the monastic site, enjoy scenic walks along well-marked trails, and enjoy the peaceful atmosphere of this ancient valley. The Glendalough Visitor Centre is home to exhibits and information about the history and significance of the site.

WHY VISIT?

Glendalough is renowned for its stunning landscapes, ancient monastic ruins, and beautiful walking trails. The perfect destination for history enthusiasts, nature lovers, and hikers, you can immerse yourself in Ireland's spiritual and scenic heritage.

County Wicklow

GETTING THERE
Accessible by car with parking available at the visitor centre; also reachable by bus from Dublin.

FUN FACT!
The round tower at Glendalough, standing 33 metres (108 ft) tall, served as a landmark for pilgrims and a refuge during attacks.

Beauty Score ★★★★★
Historical Score ★★★★★
Cultural Score ★★★★☆

Lough Tay

Marvel at one of Ireland's most picturesque lakes, resembling a pint of Guinness.

OVERVIEW
Lough Tay is a small but exceptionally picturesque lake on the private Guinness Estate in County Wicklow. Surrounded by the rugged landscape of the Wicklow Mountains, the lake is framed by steep cliffs and lush green hills. Nicknamed 'Guinness Lake', Lough Tay is known for its dark peaty waters and white sandy beach at its northern shore, resembling the head of a pint of Guinness. Access to the lake itself is restricted as it is on private property. However, visitors can enjoy stunning views from the nearby R759 road and several other vantage points along the Wicklow Way. The area offers fantastic opportunities for hiking, photography, and immersing yourself in the serene natural environment.

BEST TIME TO VISIT
April to September for optimal weather and to fully appreciate the lake's beauty and the surrounding landscape.

GETTING THERE
Accessible by car via the R759 road; parking is available at designated viewpoints.

Beauty Score ★★★★★
Historical Score ★★★☆☆
Cultural Score ★★★☆☆

WHY VISIT?
Lough Tay, also known as the 'Guinness Lake', is a stunningly beautiful lake in the heart of the Wicklow Mountains. Its dark waters and sandy shoreline resemble a pint of Guinness, making it one of Ireland's most iconic natural attractions. Lough Tay is a must-visit for scenic drives and photography, as one of the best places to appreciate Ireland's natural beauty.

FUN FACT!
Lough Tay is located on the Guinness Estate, owned by the famous Guinness family, known for their iconic Irish stout.

County Wicklow

Wicklow Way

Embark on a journey along Ireland's oldest long-distance walking trail.

OVERVIEW
Established in 1980, the Wicklow Way is Ireland's first waymarked long-distance walking trail. Starting in Marlay Park, Dublin, the trail winds through the heart of the Wicklow Mountains to the village of Clonegal in County Carlow. Hikers will encounter rolling hills, dense forests, tranquil lakes, and dramatic mountain scenery along the route. Some of the best bits are the lush valleys of Glendalough, the stunning views from the top of Djouce Mountain, and the historic ruins of ancient monastic sites. The trail is well-marked and can be tackled in sections or as a complete journey. There are also numerous accommodation options available along the way.

Beauty Score ★★★★★
Historical Score ★★★★☆
Cultural Score ★★★★☆

WHY VISIT?
The Wicklow Way is an iconic 131 km (81.4 miles) trail that traverses the Wicklow Mountains. Offering breathtaking views, varied terrain, and a journey through some of Ireland's most beautiful natural and cultural landscapes, it's perfect for hikers, nature lovers, and anyone looking to explore the beauty of Ireland on foot.

FUN FACT!
The Wicklow Way was inspired by the Appalachian Trail in the United States to highlight the beauty and diversity of the Irish landscape.

GETTING THERE
Easily accessible from Dublin, with the starting point at Marlay Park. Public transportation and parking are available at various points.

County Wicklow

Carnivan Beach

A secluded beach with golden sands and rugged coastal views.

WHY VISIT?
Carnivan Beach is a hidden gem along Ireland's sunny southeast coast. With its pristine sands, dramatic cliffs, and peaceful atmosphere, it's ideal for those seeking a quiet escape, whether for a stroll, a picnic, or water activities like swimming and surfing.

FUN FACT!
Carnivan Beach is part of Ireland's Ancient East and offers views of both County Wexford and neighbouring County Waterford.

County Wexford

OVERVIEW
Nestled on the Wexford coastline, Carnivan Beach offers an idyllic retreat away from the crowds. Known for its unspoiled beauty and tranquil surroundings, the beach is a popular spot for families, nature enthusiasts, and photographers. The area is steeped in history, with nearby ruins of an ancient church adding a sense of mystery. During low tide, rock pools are revealed, perfect for exploring marine life. Its remote location ensures a peaceful visit, making it one of County Wexford's most charming coastal destinations.

BEST TIME TO VISIT
Summer for warmer weather and autumn for a quiet, scenic retreat.

TOP FACT
The nearby ruins of Carnivan Church are said to date back to the 12th century and are rumoured to be haunted.

ACCOMMODATION TIPS
Stay in a coastal B&B in Ballygarrett or book a holiday cottage nearby for stunning sea views.

Beauty Score ★★★★★
Historical Score ★★★☆☆
Cultural Score ★★★☆☆

CONNACHT

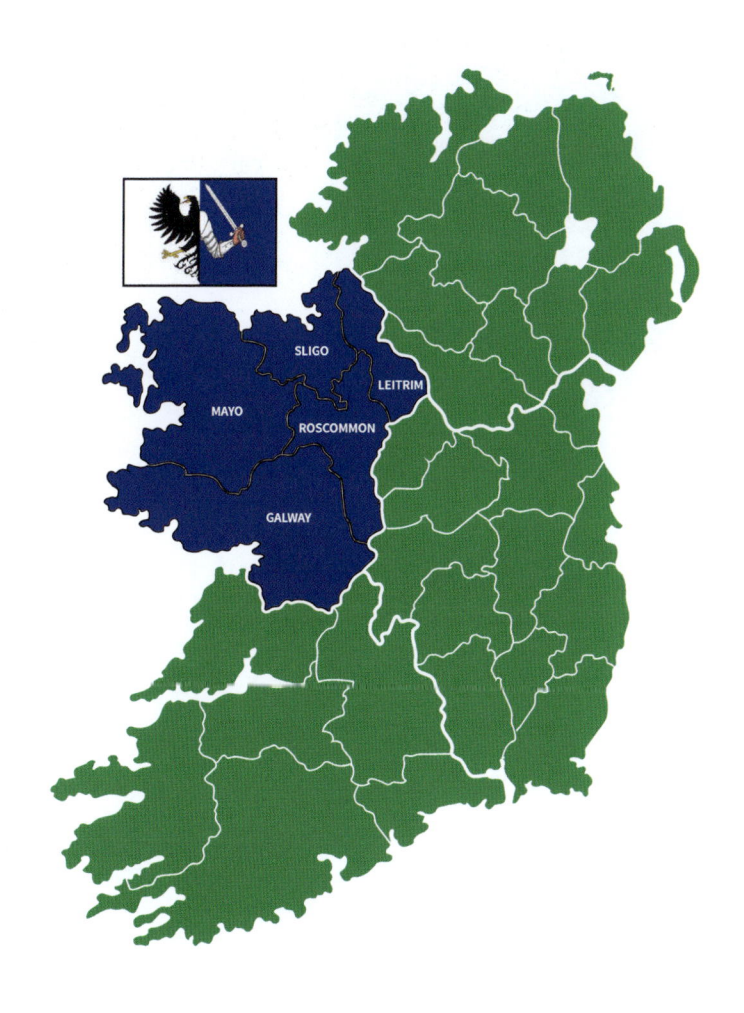

Glencar Waterfall

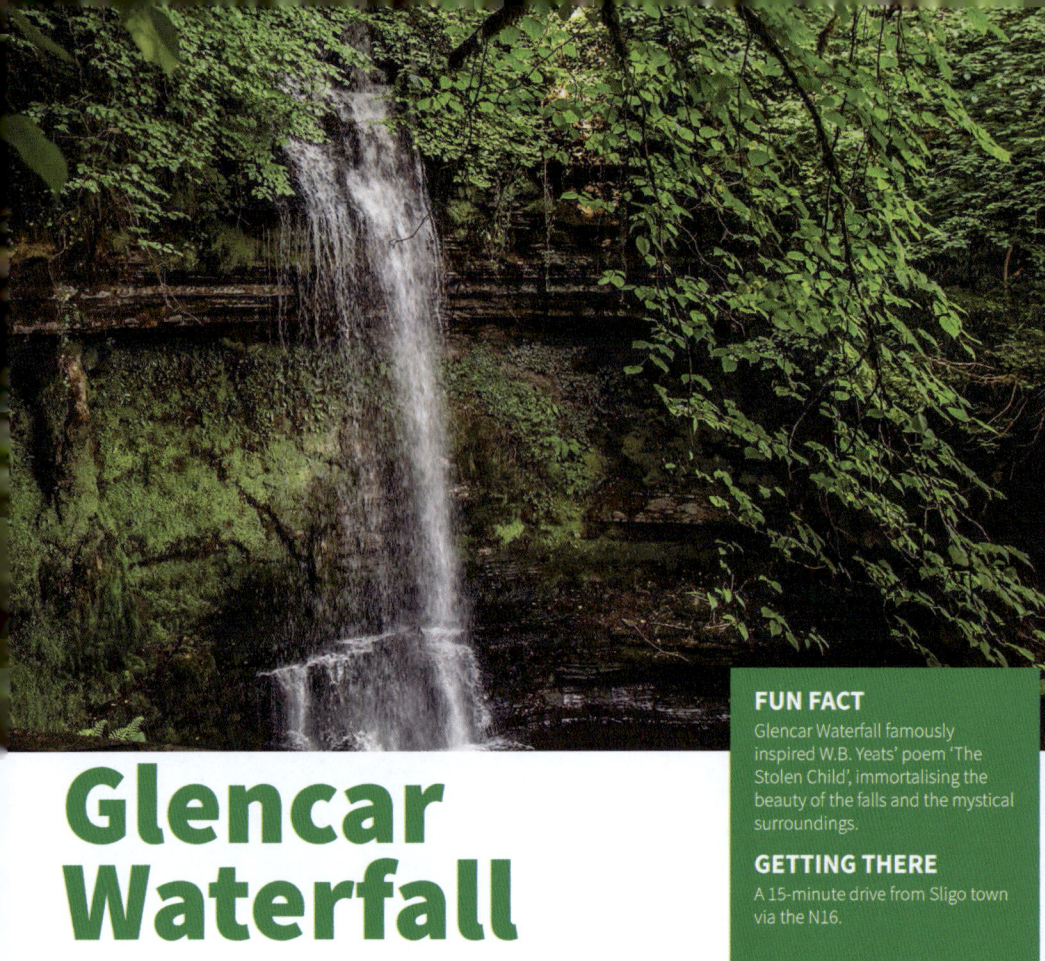

A stunning 50 ft waterfall set in lush woodland.

OVERVIEW
Nestled in the heart of County Leitrim, Glencar Waterfall is easily accessed from nearby Sligo. Sitting just a short walk from the road through a tranquil forest path, the waterfall is particularly stunning after rain, set amongst the beautiful surroundings of lush greenery and ferns. Facilities include a picnic area, playground, and café, making it an excellent spot for families and nature lovers.

WHY VISIT
Glencar Waterfall is one of Ireland's most picturesque natural attractions, tumbling gracefully from a height of 50 feet (15.24 m) into a serene pool below. Its beauty inspired Irish poet W.B. Yeats, who mentioned it in his famous poem 'The Stolen Child'. The peaceful surroundings and gentle walking trails make it perfect for a relaxing day spent in nature.

LOCAL LEGEND
Local folklore speaks of fairies living in the area, with Glencar's mystical atmosphere drawing many who believe in Ireland's ancient legends.

FUN FACT
Glencar Waterfall famously inspired W.B. Yeats' poem 'The Stolen Child', immortalising the beauty of the falls and the mystical surroundings.

GETTING THERE
A 15-minute drive from Sligo town via the N16.

Beauty Score ★★★★★
Historical Score ★★★☆☆
Cultural Score ★★★★☆

County Leitrim

Connemara National Park

Beauty Score ★★★★★
Historical Score ★★★★☆
Cultural Score ★★★★☆

Explore Ireland's rugged wilderness with stunning landscapes, diverse wildlife, and scenic hiking trails.

WHY VISIT?
Connemara National Park offers a breathtaking experience of Ireland's rugged natural beauty, with its bogs, grasslands, woodlands, and heaths. Visitors can partake in various outdoor activities, including hiking, birdwatching, and exploring historical ruins. The park is ideal for both nature lovers and adventure seekers.

GETTING THERE
Accessible by car from Galway City (about 90 minutes), with parking available at the visitor centre in Letterfrack.

FUN FACT!
Connemara National Park is home to the Connemara pony, a native Irish breed known for its agility and friendly temperament.

County Galway

OVERVIEW
Spanning 2,957 hectares of scenic mountains, heaths, grasslands, and bogs, Connemara National Park is a haven for wildlife. The park's highest peak, Diamond Hill, offers spectacular views and panoramas of the surrounding landscape and coastline. Visitors can explore several marked trails of varying difficulties, enjoy the visitor centre's exhibits, and learn about the region's natural and cultural history. The park also includes the ruins of a 19th-century graveyard, ancient megalithic tombs, and 4,000-year-old Neolithic artefacts.

BEST TIME TO VISIT
Late Spring to early autumn (April to September) for the best weather and full access to the castle grounds.

Aran Islands

Beauty Score ★★★★★
Historical Score ★★★★★
Cultural Score ★★★★☆

FUN FACT!
The Aran Islands are known for the iconic Aran sweaters, traditionally knitted by islanders and recognised worldwide for their intricate patterns and craftsmanship.

GETTING THERE
Accessible by ferry from Rossaveal (near Galway) or Doolin (County Clare) and by air from Connemara Airport.

BEST TIME TO VSIT
Late Spring to early autumn (May to September) for the best weather and ferry services.

County Galway

Experience the rugged beauty and unique cultural heritage of Ireland's west coast.

OVERVIEW
The Aran Islands are located off the coast of County Galway and are accessible by ferry from Rossaveal or by air from Connemara Airport. Inis Mór, the largest island, is home to the ancient fort of Dún Aonghasa, which sits perched on a cliff edge. Inis Meáin, the middle island, offers a quieter, more traditional experience, while Inis Oírr, the smallest island, features sandy beaches and a shipwreck. The islands are a haven for those seeking tranquillity, with plenty of opportunities for hiking, cycling, and exploring the rich flora and fauna.

WHY VISIT?
The Aran Islands blend natural beauty, ancient history, and rich cultural traditions. Comprising three islands – Inis Mór, Inis Meáin, and Inis Oírr – the Aran Islands are known for their dramatic landscapes, iconic stone walls, and well-preserved archaeological sites. Visitors can explore the islands by bike, foot, or pony and trap and immerse themselves in the traditional Irish-speaking communities off the coast of Galway.

Dunguaire Castle

Witness Ireland's most picturesque coastal castle.

OVERVIEW
Dunguaire Castle, built in 1520, stands proudly near the charming village of Kinvara. This beautifully restored tower house boasts a rich history and stunning views of Galway Bay, making it an absolute must-visit. The castle hosts medieval banquets where guests can dine like Irish nobility while enjoying tales of Irish folklore. A visit to Dunguaire offers an enchanting experience, with a peaceful setting that is ideal for photographers, history enthusiasts, and anyone looking for a cultural escape.

WHY VISIT?
Perched on the edge of Galway Bay, Dunguaire Castle is one of Ireland's most iconic and picturesque castles. It offers visitors a glimpse into medieval Irish life, boasting an immersive experience of history and culture through seasonal banquets, thoughtful exhibits, and scenic coastal surroundings.

FUN FACT!
Dunguaire Castle is said to have been built on the site of the ancient palace of the legendary King Guaire, from whom the castle takes its name.

Beauty Score   ★★★★★
Historical Score   ★★★★★
Cultural Score   ★★★★☆

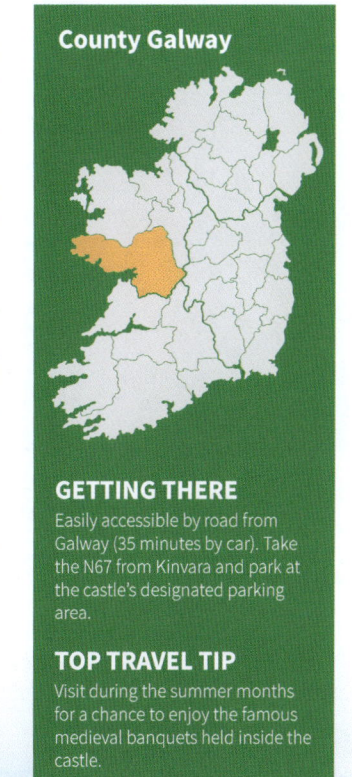

County Galway

GETTING THERE
Easily accessible by road from Galway (35 minutes by car). Take the N67 from Kinvara and park at the castle's designated parking area.

TOP TRAVEL TIP
Visit during the summer months for a chance to enjoy the famous medieval banquets held inside the castle.

Croagh Patrick

Beauty Score ★★★★★
Historical Score ★★★★☆
Cultural Score ★★★★★

Climb Ireland's holiest mountain for breathtaking views and spiritual significance.

OVERVIEW

Croagh Patrick, also known as 'The Reek', stands at 764 metres (2,507 feet) and is one of Ireland's most iconic mountains. Located near Westport in County Mayo, it has been an important pilgrimage site for over 1,500 years. Every year, especially on Reek Sunday (the last Sunday in July), thousands of pilgrims and hikers climb to the summit barefoot, where you can find a small chapel dedicated to Saint Patrick. The climb is challenging, with a steep and rocky path, but the panoramic views from the top are more than worth the effort. The mountain offers a unique combination of physical challenge, natural beauty, and spiritual fulfilment.

WHY VISIT?

Croagh Patrick is renowned for its religious significance and is believed to be where Saint Patrick fasted for forty days. It offers a challenging but rewarding hike with stunning views of Clew Bay and the surrounding landscape. It's a pilgrimage site and a natural wonder rolled into one.

FUN FACT!

On the last Sunday in July, known as 'Reek Sunday', it's traditional for some pilgrims to climb Croagh Patrick barefoot as an act of penance.

GETTING THERE

Accessible by car, with parking available at the base in the village of Murrisk. The base is also reachable by bus from Westport.

County Mayo

97

Doolough Valley

Experience the poignant history of one of Ireland's most famous valleys.

OVERVIEW
Doolough Valley is nestled between the Mweelrea and Sheeffry Hills. A place of striking natural beauty and historical significance, it is a must-visit for those visiting County Mayo. The valley is home to two glacial lakes, Doo Lough and Fin Lough, which reflect the surrounding mountains in their clear waters. The area is ideal for cycling, hiking, and scenic drives. Doolough Valley is also known for the Doolough Tragedy of 1849, a harrowing event from the Great Famine when many men, women, and children perished while seeking food and aid. A stone memorial cross stands in the valley to commemorate the victims, making it a poignant place of reflection and remembrance.

BEST TIME TO VISIT
Late Spring to early autumn (April to September) for the best weather and visibility.

GETTING THERE
Accessible by car via the R335 road from Louisburgh or Leenane; parking is available throughout the valley.

Beauty Score   ★★★★★
Historical Score ★★★★☆
Cultural Score ★★★☆☆

WHY VISIT?
Doolough Valley is renowned for its breathtaking scenery, with rugged mountains and serene lakes surrounding the valley. The site also has a tragic history, adding particular poignancy to this beautiful natural site. It is a perfect destination for hikers, photographers, and those seeking a reflective and peaceful experience.

FUN FACT!
The Doolough Tragedy is commemorated annually with a walk that retraces the steps of those who perished.

County Mayo

98

Downpatrick Head

FUN FACT!
Dun Briste sea stack was separated from the mainland during a storm in 1393, creating the dramatic formation we see today.

GETTING THERE
Accessible by car with parking near the site; local town buses also service the area.

BEST TIME TO VSIT
Late Spring to early autumn (April to September) for the best weather and visibility.

County Mayo

Witness a dramatic sea stack at one of Ireland's most iconic headlands.

OVERVIEW
Downpatrick Head is a striking headland located just a few kilometres north of Ballycastle in County Mayo. Named after Saint Patrick, who is said to have visited the area, the headland offers views of the iconic Dun Briste sea stack, which stands 50 metres (164 ft) in height and is home to numerous seabirds. The area is also home to the EIRE 64 sign, a World War II aerial navigation marker, and the ruins of an ancient church and stone cross. Visitors can enjoy walking along the cliffs, taking in breathtaking ocean views and vistas of the surrounding landscape. The blowholes and sea caves add to the dramatic scenery, making Downpatrick Head a must-visit for every kind of traveller.

WHY VISIT?
Downpatrick Head offers stunning views of the Atlantic Ocean, as well as impressive cliffs and the spectacular Dun Briste sea stack. It's a site of natural beauty, historical significance, and geological wonder, making it perfect for nature enthusiasts, photographers, and history buffs.

Beauty Score ★★★★★
Historical Score ★★★★☆
Cultural Score ★★★☆☆

Keel Beach

One of Ireland's most beautiful beaches with breathtaking coastal views.

OVERVIEW

Keel Beach is a magnificent 3.4 km (2.1 miles) stretch of sand and surf on Achill Island, known for its breathtaking scenery and vibrant outdoor activities. Ideal for watersports, including surfing, windsurfing, and kayaking, thanks to the consistent Atlantic waves, the beach is the perfect spot for families. The nearby Keel Sandybanks is a popular camping and caravan spot, providing facilities for families and adventure seekers of all kinds. Acting as a gateway to the stunning Achill Head, where hikers can explore trails with panoramic views, there is plenty to experience here. Boasting natural beauty and abundant activities, Keel Beach is a must-visit destination on Achill Island.

WHY VISIT?

Keel Beach is a pristine Blue Flag beach set against the dramatic backdrop of the Minaun Cliffs and Slievemore Mountain. Perfect for swimming, surfing, windsurfing, and enjoying the scenic natural beauty of Achill Island.

FUN FACT!

Due to its stunning and dramatic landscapes, Keel Beach has been used as a location for several films and TV series.

County Mayo

Beauty Score ★★★★★
Historical Score ★★★☆☆
Cultural Score ★★★☆☆

GETTING THERE

Accessible by car with ample parking available behind the beach. You can also get there by bus from Westport to Achill Island.

100

Keem Bay

Beauty Score ★★★★★
Historical Score ★★★☆☆
Cultural Score ★★★★☆

Discover one of Ireland's most picturesque beaches for pristine waters and dramatic coastal scenery.

WHY VISIT?
Keem Bay is a stunning and secluded beach offering pristine white sands, turquoise waters, and breathtaking views. It's perfect for swimming, snorkelling, and embracing the beauty of nature.

GETTING THERE
Accessible by car via a scenic drive along the R319; a small parking area is also located near the beach, but it can get crowded during peak season.

FUN FACT!
Keem Bay was named 'Ireland's Best Beach' by the Irish Independent and is often ranked among the top beaches in Ireland and Europe.

EXTRA FUN FACT!
The beach was used as a filming location for the film The Banshees of Inisherin. The house overlooking the bay served as the home of Colm, the character played by Colin Farrell.

County Mayo

OVERVIEW
Keem Bay, located at the western end of Achill Island, is one of Ireland's most beautiful hidden gems. Achill Island, a horseshoe-shaped bay surrounded by steep cliffs and rolling hills, boasts a dramatic and secluded coastal setting. The beach is perfect for swimming and snorkelling, with clear waters revealing a rich aquatic world. Keem Bay is also an excellent spot for walking and hiking, with the Croaghaun Cliffs that tower overhead offering panoramic views of the Atlantic Ocean and the surrounding island landscape. Historically, the Bay was a key site for basking shark fishing, and remnants of the old watch house can still be seen. Keem Bay offers a truly memorable experience whether you're seeking adventure or relaxation.

Roscommon Castle

A 13th-century ruin steeped in Irish history.

OVERVIEW

Roscommon Castle was built in 1269 by the Normans. Today, it stands as a hauntingly beautiful ruin in Roscommon Town. Its imposing structure, though partially destroyed during the Cromwellian conquest, still stands tall amid serene parklands. Visitors can walk through the ruins, admire the rugged architecture, and enjoy the peaceful surrounding lakes and green spaces, which are perfect for picnics or enjoying a relaxing afternoon.

WHY VISIT?

Roscommon Castle offers a unique opportunity to explore the ruins of a once-mighty 13th-century Norman fortress. Surrounded by tranquil parklands, the castle tells the story of Ireland's turbulent history through its weathered stones. Thus, making it a perfect spot for history lovers, photographers, and families looking for a scenic stroll.

County Roscommon

GETTING THERE

From the Roscommon town square, head north and take the exit for Castle Street. Take a left down Castle Lane, where you can park and walk a short distance to the castle. You can also reach the Castle via public transport.

FUN FACT!

The castle changed hands multiple times between Irish and English forces during the 16th century, reflecting its strategic importance.

Beauty Score ★★★★☆
Historical Score ★★★★★
Cultural Score ★★★★☆

Benbulben

Beauty Score ★★★★★
Historical Score ★★★★☆
Cultural Score ★★★★★

Marvel at the iconic flat-topped peak of Benbulben, known for its beauty and folklore.

OVERVIEW

Benbulben is a large and distinctive rock formation in the Dartry Mountains in County Sligo. Formed during the Ice Age, this majestic mountain offers several scenic hiking trails that provide panoramic views of the Irish landscape, including the Atlantic Ocean, surrounding valleys, and lush green fields. The mountain is also steeped in Irish mythology and literature, with connections to the legendary warrior Fionn MacCumhaill and the poet W.B. Yeats, who is buried nearby at Drumcliffe Churchyard. The site also features diverse flora and fauna, making it a haven for biodiversity and a perfect spot for nature photography.

WHY VISIT?

Benbulben is often referred to as Ireland's Table Mountain. It boasts unique geological formations, stunning views, and a significant cultural history. It's an ideal destination for hikers, nature lovers, and those interested in Irish mythology.

FUN FACT!

Benbulben's flat-topped summit makes it one of Ireland's most recognisable mountains, often compared to Table Mountain in South Africa.

GETTING THERE

Accessible by car with parking available at designated trailheads; public transport options are limited.

County Sligo

Medb's Cairn

Hike to the summit of Knocknarea to see the neolithic Queen Medb's Cairn.

OVERVIEW
Medb's Cairn sits atop Knocknarea, a prominent hill near Sligo town. The massive stone cairn, which measures 55 metres (180 ft) wide and 10 metres (32.8 ft) high, is believed to be the burial place of Queen Medb, a legendary figure from Irish mythology. The hike to the summit of Knocknarea takes approximately two hours to complete and provides spectacular views of the Atlantic Ocean, Sligo Bay, and the surrounding countryside. Along the way, you'll encounter other ancient sites and enjoy the region's natural beauty.

BEST TIME TO VISIT
Morning or late afternoon for the best light and fewer crowds.

GETTING THERE
The summit is accessible by car, and parking is available at the base of Knocknarea. The short hike starts from the car park.

LOCAL LEGEND
According to legend, Queen Medb was slain by a slingshot from Furbaide Ferbend, who sought revenge for his mother, Clothru, Medb's own sister.

Beauty Score ★★★★★
Historical Score ★★★★☆
Cultural Score ★★★★★

WHY VISIT?
Medb's Cairn offers stunning natural beauty, panoramic views, and deep historical and mythological significance. The hike to the cairn offers a rewarding physical challenge and a journey through Ireland's rich past.

FUN FACT!
According to legend, Queen Medb was buried upright in the cairn, facing her enemies in Ulster.

County Sligo

Voya Seaweed Baths

Experience the therapeutic benefits of organic seaweed bathing in a tranquil seaside setting.

OVERVIEW

Voya Seaweed Baths, located in the picturesque village of Strandhill, provide a luxurious and natural spa experience that uses sustainably harvested seaweed. A trip to the baths involves immersing yourself in warm seawater infused with seaweed, known for its detoxifying and moisturising properties. This traditional Irish treatment has been used for centuries to alleviate skin conditions, reduce inflammation, and promote overall well-being. The spa also offers a range of other treatments, including massages, facials, and body scrubs, all using organic seaweed-based products. With its calming atmosphere and stunning coastal views, Voya Seaweed Baths offer a perfect escape for relaxation and rejuvenation.

WHY VISIT?

Voya Seaweed Baths offer a natural and uniquely Irish spa experience that utilises the healing properties of hand-harvested organic seaweed from the Atlantic Ocean. It's perfect for those seeking relaxation, wellness treatments, and a connection to nature in a serene coastal environment.

GETTING THERE

Accessible by car with parking available; also reachable by bus from Sligo town.

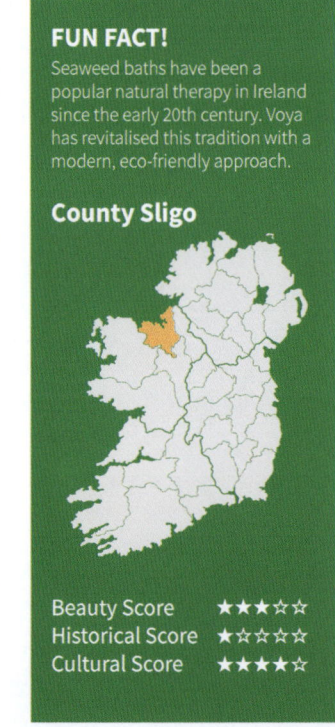

FUN FACT!

Seaweed baths have been a popular natural therapy in Ireland since the early 20th century. Voya has revitalised this tradition with a modern, eco-friendly approach.

County Sligo

Beauty Score ★★★☆☆
Historical Score ★☆☆☆☆
Cultural Score ★★★★☆

105

Credits and Copyright

101 places to see in Ireland before you die

This book would not exist without the incredible dedication of the team and the talented photographers who brought it to life. For more insights into Ireland's best experiences, check out **irelandbeforeyoudie.com**. For any questions about this book, email **info@irelandbeforeyoudie.com**.

Editor: Sian McQuillan | **Designer:** Brian Opole

Image Credits:

Ulster:

Carrick-A-Rede Rope Bridge: Left image: Carrick-a-Rede Rope Bridge by Graham Hogg, licensed under CC BY-SA 2.0. Causeway Coastal Route: Left image: Causeway Coastal Route by Jennifer Boyer, licensed under CC BY 2.0, via Flickr. Dunluce Castle: Left image: Dunluce Castle by James O'Keefe, licensed under CC BY 2.0, via Flickr. Glenoe Waterfall: Bottom image: Glenoe Waterfall by Ross, licensed under CC BY-SA 2.0, via Wikimedia Commons. Rathlin Island: Bottom image: Rathlin Island Cliffs and Caves by Chris Brooks, licensed under CC BY-SA 2.0, via Flickr. The Dark Hedges: Bottom image: The Dark Hedges by Colin Park, licensed under CC BY-SA 2.0, via Wikimedia Commons. Bushmills Distillery: Bottom image: Old Bushmills Distillery by Dr Neil Clifton, licensed under CC BY-SA 2.0, via Wikimedia Commons. The Crosskeys Inn: Bottom image: The Crosskeys Inn by Brian Morrison, via Ireland's Content Pool. Carrickfergus Castle: Bottom image: Carrickfergus Castle by Donna from Belfast, licensed under CC BY 2.0, via Wikimedia Commons. Crumlin Road Gaol: Bottom image: Crumlin Road Gaol by Z Thomas, licensed under CC BY-SA 4.0, via Wikimedia Commons. Galgorm: Bottom image: Galgorm Resort & Spa, image courtesy of Galgorm, via galgorm.com. Navan Fort & Visitor Centre: Bottom image: Navan Fort and Centre, courtesy of Navan Centre and Fort, via Ireland's Content Pool. Dún na Rí Forest Park: Bottom image: "Lady's Lake" in Dún na Rí Forest Park by D Gore, licensed under CC BY-SA 2.0, via Wikimedia Commons. Halloween in Derry: Bottom image: Derry Girls Halloween Mural by Greg Clarke, licensed under CC BY-SA 2.0, via Flickr. The City Walls: Top image: Derry Walls – Double Bastion by Otter, licensed under CC BY-SA 4.0, via Wikimedia Commons. Bottom image: Cannons on the Derry city walls by N Chadwick, licensed under CC BY-SA 2.0, via Wikimedia Commons. Mussenden Temple: Top image: Mussenden Temple by Kent Wang, licensed under CC BY 2.0, via Flickr. Bottom image: Mussenden Temple by D LN, licensed under CC BY-SA 4.0, via Wikimedia Commons. Malin Head: Top image: Malin Head by Kent Wang, licensed under CC BY 2.0, via Flickr. Bottom image: Malin Head, Donegal, by Giuseppe Milo, licensed under CC BY 2.0, via Wikimedia Commons. The Slieve League Cliffs: Image: Slieve League by Kent Wang, licensed under CC BY 2.0, via Flickr. Ballymastocker Beach: Image: Ballymastocker Bay by Philip McErlean, licensed under CC BY 2.0, via Flickr. Glenveagh National Park: Image: Glenveagh National Park by Anna & Michal, licensed under CC BY 2.0, via Flickr. Tory Island: Image: Tory Island Early Medieval Ecclesiastical Site by Julianne Forde, licensed under CC BY-SA 4.0, via Wikimedia Commons. The Glenevin Waterfall: Image: Glenevin Waterfall by Maxima, via GoodFon. Mourne Mountains: Image: Slieve Donard by Dieglop, licensed under CC BY-SA 4.0, via Wikimedia Commons. Murlough Beach: Image: Murlough Strand from the sand dunes by Eric Jones, licensed under CC BY-SA 2.0, via Wikimedia Commons. Mount Stewart: Image: Mount Stewart by Sitomon, licensed under CC BY-SA 2.0, via Wikimedia Commons. Cuilcagh Mountain Park: Image: Cuilcagh, Fermanagh by Carl Meehan, licensed under CC BY 2.0, via Flickr. Marble Arch Caves: Image: Marble Arch Caves by Paul Lindsay, courtesy of Marble Arch Caves, via Ireland's Content Pool. Rally School Ireland: Image: Rally School Ireland, via Facebook. Ulster American Folk Park: Image: Ulster American Folk Park by Kenneth Allen, licensed under CC BY-SA 2.0, via Geograph.

Munster:

Aillwee Cave: Top image: Aillwee Cave by N Chadwick, courtesy of Geograph, via Creative Commons. Bottom image: Aillwee Cave Waterfall by MarvinVells, licensed under CC BY-SA 3.0, via Wikimedia Commons. Dursey Island: Top image: Signal Tower, Dursey Island by Cathy Cox, courtesy of Geograph, via Creative Commons. Bottom image: Dursey Island Cable Car by K. Jähne, licensed under CC BY-SA 3.0, via Wikimedia Commons. Spike Island: Image: Spike Island by Guliolopez, licensed under CC BY-SA 3.0, via Wikimedia Commons. Brow Head: Top image: Brow Head by Jonathan Billinger, licensed under CC BY-SA 2.0, via Geograph. Bottom image: Signal Tower, Brow Head by Richard Webb, licensed under CC BY-SA 2.0, via Geograph. Cobh: Image: Cobh Cathedral by Chris Hill, © Tourism Ireland, via Ireland's Content Pool. Fota Wildlife Park: Top image: Fota Island Wildlife Park by Chris Hill, © Tourism Ireland, via Ireland's Content Pool. Bottom image: Eastern Grey Kangaroo at Fota Wildlife Park by William Murphy, licensed under CC BY-SA 2.0, via Flickr. Carrauntoohil: Image: Carrauntoohil by John Doyle, via Unsplash. Ross Castle: Image: Ross Castle, Killarney National Park by Robert Linsdell, licensed under CC BY 2.0, via Wikimedia Commons.

Leinster:

Duckett's Grove: Image: Duckett's Grove by michelleronan, licensed under CC BY-SA 4.0, via Wikimedia Commons. Castletown House: Bottom left image: Castletown House by Digging3pace, licensed under CC BY SA 4.0, via Wikimedia Commons. Bottom right image: Castletown House, Celbridge by RafalZabron, licensed under CC BY-SA 4.0, via Wikimedia Commons. Kilmainham Gaol: Image: Kilmainham Gaol courtesy of Tourism Ireland, via Ireland's Content Pool. The Guinness Storehouse: Image courtesy of Diageo Ireland Brand Homes.

Connacht:

Glendalough: Top image: Upper Lake in Glendalough by R.undefined, licensed under CC BY-SA 4.0, via Wikimedia Commons. Bottom image: Glendalough by J.-H. Janßen, licensed under CC BY-SA 3.0, via Wikimedia Commons. Lough Tay: Image: Lough Tay by Chris Hill, © Fáilte Ireland/Tourism Ireland. Glencar Waterfall: Image: Glencar Waterfall by Wikimedia Commons, licensed under CC BY-SA. Croagh Patrick: Top image: Statue of St. Patrick at the footstep of Croagh Patrick by Tom Szustek, licensed under CC BY-SA 4.0, via Wikimedia Commons. Bottom image: Croagh Patrick by Mal B, licensed under CC BY, via Flickr. Benbulben: Image: Benbulben by Tourism Ireland, via Ireland's Content Pool. Voya Seaweed Baths: Image: Voya Seaweed Baths, via Voya Seaweed Baths on Facebook.

Copyright © 2025

Printed in Great Britain
by Amazon